Marbling Paper & Fabric

CAROL TAYLOR

*with Patty Schleicher,
Mimi Schleicher &
Laura Sims*

A Sterling/Lark Book
Sterling Publishing Co., Inc.   New York

Design: Marcia Winters
Production: Marcia Winters
    and Elaine Thompson
Photography: Evan Bracken
Editorial Assistance: Dawn Cusick
Illustrations: Donald Osby
    (Tray Illustration by David Withrington)
Cover Design: Karen Nelson

Library of Congress Cataloging-in-Publication Data
Taylor, Carol, 1943-
    Marbling paper and fabric / Carol Taylor with Patty Schleicher,
Mimi Schleicher, Laura Sims ; (photography, Evan Bracken ;
illustrations, Donald Osby).
        p.   cm.
    "A Sterling/Lark book."
    Includes bibliographical references and index.
    ISBN 0-8069-8322-1
    1. Marbling (Bookbinding) 2. Marbling. I. Title
Z271.3.M37T38   1990
    686.3'6–dc20   90-24772
                                                    CIP

10 9 8 7 6 5 4 3 2 1

A Sterling/Lark Book

Produced by Altamont Press, Inc.
50 College Street, Asheville, NC 28801

First paperback edition published in 1992 by
Sterling Publishing Company, Inc.
387 Park Avenue South, New York, N.Y. 10016

© 1991 by Altamont Press

Distributed in Canada by Sterling Publishing
% Canadian Manda Group, P.O. Box 920, Station U
Toronto, Ontario, Canada M8Z 5P9
Distributed in Great Britain and Europe by Cassell PLC
Villiers House, 41/47 Strand, London WC2N 5JE, England
Distributed in Australia by Capricorn Link Ltd.
P.O. Box 665, Lane Cove, NSW 2066

Every effort has been made to ensure that all the information
in this book is accurate. However, due to differing conditions,
tools, and individual skills, the publisher cannot be responsible
for any injuries, losses, and other damages which may result
from the use of the information in this book.

Sterling   ISBN 0-8069-8322-1   Trade
                    0-8069-8323-X   Paper

PREFACE

When one author and three creative consultants have worked on a book together for months, it is difficult to remember precisely who contributed exactly what. (The only thing clear from first to last is that the author was *always* outnumbered.) Still, responsibility can be divided up in at least general terms.

I'm a professional writer and editor who is in love with marbling. Patty Schleicher, Mimi Schleicher, and Laura Sims are professional marblers who are in love with books. In a leap of the imagination, we decided to combine our affections and our skills to produce a book about marbling.

Predictably, the words are mine. The marbling—the precision of line, the fluidity of pattern—is theirs. Their detailed, practical expertise has added immeasurably to this book.

I'm pleased with the marbling and they're pleased with the text, which probably explains why we all still like each other. We sincerely hope you'll be pleased with both.

CONTENTS

INTRODUCTION

▰▰▰▰▰▰▰▰▰▰▰▰

Marbling is an ancient craft that has captivated Turkish sultans and French peasants, Japanese emperors and American hippies. Why has it charmed so many for so long?

First, there's the color—color so rich and deep that a marbled page glows in the lamplight; and color as light and subtle as the silk scarf it adorns.

Second, there are the patterns—simple, angular patterns that are obvious at once; and patterns so complex that they are invisible at first, emerging only gradually from a thousand details.

Third, there's the water—the essential medium of the craft. A marbled surface is a brilliant record of moving water, of currents, eddies, and swirls.

All this complexity flows from a simple process. To marble a piece of paper, you thicken a shallow pan of water and float paint across its surface. Using simple rakes and combs, you swirl the paint into patterns, lay the paper on top, pick it up, and rinse it off. The pattern that was on the surface of the water is now on the paper.

In other words, marbling is, quite literally, child's play. Ten-year-olds learn to do it in an afternoon, and they love it. "It's magic!" they cry, as they lift a bright piece of paper or a raucous T-shirt from the pan.

Yet marbling can intrigue an adult for a lifetime. At first you marble everything within reach in your favorite colors and in simple patterns. Then you get restless. You begin to experiment with complicated patterns and with colors you've never cared about before. One day you realize that your sense of color has sharpened—that you actually see better. You notice subtler shades, careful gradations of less obvious hues. You spend a ridiculous amount of time thinking about the interplay among colors and the interaction between color and pattern.

You're hooked. And marbling still feels like magic—every time.

This book can help you become a magician. In it you'll find all the information you need to marble paper and fabric—and a few tips for marbling wood. You'll also find 36 answers to the inevitable question of someone who's just produced a lovely piece of marbled paper or fabric—"What can I do with this?

There is an enormous range of expertise in the craft of marbling—from the child whose papers dress up the refrigerator, to the young entrepreneur who marbles T-shirts for weekend craft fairs, to the artist whose exquisite silk garments hang on gallery walls. Happily, there is room for us all.

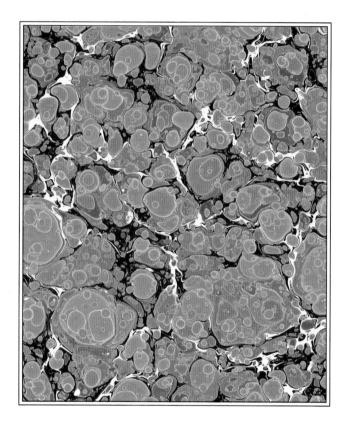

HISTORY

~~~~~~~~

Marbling takes its name from the stone prized by builders and sculptors for centuries, even before Augustus Caesar "found Rome brick and left it marble." Some of the designs on marbled paper resemble the veins and ripples in that shining stone.

The first marbling was Oriental. Early in the 12th century, Japanese artists began to decorate precious handmade paper with *suminagashi—sumi,* or "black ink," and *nagashi,* or "floating." When a brush filled with ink is lightly dipped into a tray of water, the ink floats. If a second brush containing a kind of resist, or surfactant, is dipped into the center of the ink spot, the ink expands into a larger circle. An artist can alternate the brushes until pleased with the pattern, then lay a sheet of paper on the surface of the water and lift off the design.

The delicate papers caught the fancy of Japan's royal household, which promptly outlawed their possession by anyone else. The imperial family used the papers for poetry, calligraphy, and correspondence.

The form of marbling known to the West—paints floating on a gum-thickened tank of water—originated in Turkey in the 15th century, the Golden Age of the Ottoman Empire. Known as *ebru*, or "cloud art," marbling was used for calligraphy, to border manuscripts, and to frame drawings and paintings.

The Ottomans had a better idea. Once a paper was marbled, it could not be erased without obvious marring of the design—a splendid deterrent to political enemies who might be tempted to forge or otherwise tamper with official documents. In short order, documents of state were written on marbled paper. For the system to work, knowledge of marbling had to be confined to a few court artists. As they had in Japan, the ruling powers shrouded marbling in secrecy.

This drawing from Diderot's Encyclopedie *shows marblers at work.*

In the 16th century, marbled paper traveled westward along the great trade routes to Europe, where a handful of craftsmen invented patterns still named for their country of origin: Italian Hair Vein, French Curl, Old Dutch, Spanish. Ordinary folk used the colorful

papers to decorate chimney places, line cupboards, bind books, and cover boxes (see our version, page 94).

In 18th-century France, marbling was given wider currency by the great French rationalist Denis Diderot, chief editor of the *Encyclopedie*. Appalled by a reactionary church and state that suppressed art and science, Diderot enlisted artists and men of letters from throughout France. Together they wrote an encyclopedia, a summary of art and science as they knew it, convinced that scientific information would loosen the stranglehold of superstition and dogma—a point not lost upon the church and state, which clapped Diderot into prison for three months. Nonetheless, the 28 volumes of the *Encyclopedie* were published between 1751 and 1772. Included were detailed descriptions of the art of marbling, and line drawings of marblers at work.

By the 18th century, the craft found its way to the American colonies. Marbled paper was popular for "pamphlet wrappers"— coverings for cheap books (see our version, page 114). And in pre-Revolutionary America, lots of people had a great deal to say. Benjamin Franklin bound his almanacs in marbled paper, and at his insistence the $20 bill, issued in 1776, was marbled on one of its short ends to prevent forgery.

In England knowledge of marbling was suppressed less by decree than by the determined secrecy of craftsmen themselves. By the early 19th century, books with marbled end papers were popular enough to support a thriving industry. Marbling houses operated on the apprentice system. The master would wander through the local work house in search of likely-looking boys to work long hours in exchange for what passed as bed and board. In return, he promised to teach the boys his trade. In actuality, he did no such thing. Unwilling to train his future competition, the master taught each boy only one step in the process: how to make the bath, or how to grind the paints, or how to execute a pattern. Work stations were separated by screens, so that no one could watch anyone else. When the boys completed their seven-year apprenticeship, they were turned into the streets.

The game was called by Charles Woolnough, a self-taught marbler who took a dim view of artistic secrecy in general and the exploitation of children in particular. In 1853 he braved the wrath of his fellow marblers and published *The Art of Marbling*, a textbook that described all phases of the process.

As the 19th century drew to a close and book production became mechanized, marbling faded into obscurity. No one has managed, then or now, to eliminate the individual artist from the art of marbling. It remained a curiosity in antique books until the late 1970s, when the crafts movement reminded us of the beauty of hand work and the value of taking pains.

A contemporary example of suminagashi. The original is 18" by 12" (45 by 30 cm.).

MARBLING: THE BASICS

A sk three marblers a question about their craft, and you'll get three different answers. On a good day you'll get six. Marbling is, in every sense, a fluid art.

If you adopt this craft, you must make it your own. There are general guidelines but no fixed rules, and what works for one person may fail miserably for another. You just have to jump in and get your feet, hands, and stomach wet.

On the other hand, all marblers would agree that the process involves a few indispensable steps:

- Make the size, or bath—the thickened water the paints will float on.
- Mordant the paper or fabric, so that the paint will adhere to it.
- Drop the paint onto the surface of the size, allowing the paint to float and spread out into smooth, round "stones"—flat discs of color an inch or two wide (2.5 to 5 cm.).
- Manipulate the paint into interesting patterns.
- Lay the paper or fabric on the surface, so that the paints are transferred to it.
- Rinse off the new creation and hang it to dry.
- Clean the tools and work area.

The remainder of this chapter will describe how to do each of these steps, for both paper and fabric. Along the way are a few tips and a bit of advice from creative consultants who marble for a living.

EQUIPMENT

Although most tools for marbling paper are identical to those for marbling fabric, you'll need two sets of everything if you plan to marble both. Different kinds of paint are used for paper and fabric. If tools are used interchangeably, residues of acrylic fabric paints will contaminate the paper-marbling process.

Most of the necessary equipment is probably already lying around the house—buckets, a blender, measuring spoons. Only two items are specific to marbling: a tray and a set of patterning tools. Both are easy to find or make.

A pixie face appeared when the artist swirled water-base paint across the surface of the size with a stylus.

TRAY

You'll need a waterproof tray that's two to three inches deep (5 to 7.5 cm.) and a couple of inches longer and wider than the paper or fabric you plan to marble. Wood, plastic, and stainless steel are suitable materials. It's important that the tray be white or at least light-colored, so that paint floating on the surface of the bath will be visible.

Trays (also known as tanks) can be ordered from a marbling supplier (see "Mail-Order Sources," page 127). This is an easy option but not much fun.

More satisfying are "found trays"—containers that were originally designed for something else. A disposable aluminum baking pan, a plastic dishpan, or even a baking sheet with one-inch (2.5 cm.) sides will serve for a few experimental marblings.

For the longer term, photographers' developing trays are excellent and readily available from photo-supply stores. Beekeeping suppliers

MAKING A TRAY

All you need is a waterproof box large enough to hold whatever you want to marble. A few refinements are optional.

First, the bath must be covered when not in use to keep dust off the surface. The cover can be of entirely different material—a piece of hardboard is lightweight and effective. Or, when you make the tray, cut a second piece of plywood the same size as the bottom, which will serve as a perfectly fitting cover. (It can also double as a rinse board.)

To make your life easier, add a drain hole in one corner of the bottom. It will allow you to drain out the old size without hefting around a full tank—particularly useful on fabric tanks, which tend to be larger than those designed for paper. When the tank is in use, plug the hole with a rubber sink stopper or even a wine cork. (Hint: Select the stopper first, then drill the hole to fit it.)

To make your life even easier, you can add a "slop trough," as it's elegantly known. Then, when you skim the bath—as you will before every print—the surface size can slosh over into the trough, out the drain hole, and into a bucket on the floor.

The directions here are for a 20" x 30" tray. They can be adapted for any dimensions.

Cut all the pieces from the plywood. (If you're adding a slop trough, cut one long edge of the partition at a 45° angle.) If you intend to add a drain hole, drill it near one corner of the bottom. (Take into account that in each corner 1/2" of the bottom will be covered by a side and another 1/2" by an end.)

Place one side on the bottom, and glue it in place. Repeat for ends and remaining side. While the glue is still wet, reinforce the tank with finishing

nails: nail up through the bottom into the sides and ends, and nail into the ends from the sides.

If you want a slop trough, glue the partition across the box about 3" from the end that has the drain hole. Place the partition at about a 45° angle, with angled edge on the bottom and its top sloping toward the trough. Nail through the sides of the box into the partition.

Paint the box with white polyurethane, using three or more coats along the joints and in the corners. Allow the paint to dry, and give the entire tray a final coat.

If you can't find white polyurethane, paint the tray with white enamel, and let it dry. Then apply two or three coats of clear polyurethane along the joints and corners, and let each dry. Then give the entire tray a coat of clear poly.

With either coating, when the tray is dry, fill it with water and set it in the sun for two days. This will season the tray and leach out any impurities from the paint.

Note that if you build a slop trough, the working surface is reduced by the width of the trough.

MATERIALS LIST
From 1/2" exterior-grade plywood, cut

2 sides	30" x 3"
2 ends	19" x 3"
1 bottom	20" x 30"
1 cover	20" x 30"
1 trough partition (optional)	19" x 3"

Wood glue
Galvanized finishing nails
White polyurethane, or white enamel and clear polyurethane
Rubber sink stopper or wine cork (optional)

METRIC EQUIVALENTS

1/2"	13 mm.
3"	7.5 cm.
19"	47.5 cm.
20"	50 cm.
30"	75 cm.

carry good trays. Splendid ones lurk at flea markets and garage sales. Enterprising marblers have snatched up maple sugaring trays, cat litter trays (unused), and product display tanks. ("Forget the jellies. How much for the tray they're sitting in?")

Then, of course, you can make your own. Essentially, all you need is a box—four sides and a bottom. Even the woodworking-impaired can produce one with a hammer, a saw, and some exterior-grade plywood. (For details, see "Making a Tray," on page 15.)

A "quick and dirty" solution to tank building—especially useful when you want to marble an odd-sized item—is to buy some one-by-four lumber and build a rectangular frame. Attach the board ends with flat metal angles screwed into the wood, or just nail the boards together. Line the tank with a sheet of clear plastic, and fill.

COLOR APPLICATORS

There are any number of tools for getting the paint onto the surface of the size.

Whisks. A whisk is a highly efficient color applicator, probably the most common one for paper marbling. Whisks are small bunches of broom straw, also known as "broom corn"—the stuff that brooms are made of. Broom straw is carried in a few craft stores and by most marbling suppliers. Or buy a new broom and take it apart.

Wherever you get it, cut the broom straw to a suitable length (not so long that it will topple the jar of paint it will stand in), and bind enough of it together to make a whisk about an inch thick (2.5 cm.). It can be tied together with string or just wrapped with rubber bands. Rubber bands are easier, but they do tend to disintegrate right in the middle of a complicated pattern. They should be checked regularly for wear and tear, much like automotive fan belts.

Eye droppers. They are obtainable from any drug store.

Plastic bottles. These are useful for

fabric marbling, especially when you want larger stones, which require more paint. They must have a pointed tip, so that the paint will fall in drops.

Plastic bottles are available at craft stores and at many drug stores and discount marts. Beauty supply outlets have a dozen different sizes.

PATTERN-MAKING TOOLS

While marbling suppliers sell tools for manipulating the floating paint, combs and rakes are remarkably easy to make. Moreover, homemade tools can fit your tank exactly.

To marble traditional patterns, you'll need a stylus and some combs and rakes. A stylus is any object with a single long point. Combs are implements with small teeth spaced close together. Rakes have larger teeth spaced farther apart. At what spacing a comb becomes a rake depends on which marbler you ask. For our purposes, if its teeth are an inch (2.5 cm.) or farther apart, it's a rake.

A good starting collection consists of one stylus; two combs, one with teeth a quarter-inch apart (6 mm.), the other with teeth a half-inch apart (13 mm.); and two rakes, one with teeth an inch apart (2.5 cm.), the other with teeth either two or three inches apart (5 to 7.5 cm.).

Stylus. Around every house sits a neglected implement just waiting to be recognized as a stylus: a rat-tail comb (the tail end), an Afro comb (the pick end), a wooden dowel (sharpened in a pencil sharpener), a chopstick, a knitting needle. Once you find it, it will become the one tool you can't do without. (Marblers have been overheard to demand of each other, "You use *what?*")

Combs and rakes. There are any number of ways to put these together and only a few simple requirements.

First, the tools should fit the tray. This is so basic a necessity that if in the future you get a new tray, it is

■

A yardstick makes an excellent base for a comb or rake. Not only is it lightweight and a good width, but "regular intervals" are already marked off. Or a piece of graph paper can be glued to a board.

■

A variety of pins will work for combs and rakes: straight pins, T-pins, butterfly pins, quilter's pins, drapery pins.

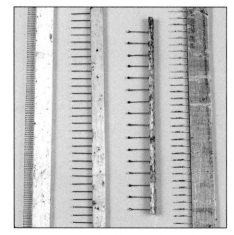

Marbling combs don't have to be pretty to produce lovely effects.

worth your time to make new tools to fit it. If the tools are too long to fit into the tray, they're obviously unusable. If they're significantly shorter than the tray, they won't comb the whole surface, which means the entire pattern will twist and distort.

To begin with, make combs to fit the width of the tank, so that you can comb up and down as you stand at one of the short ends. Eventually you may want combs to fit both directions. Make rakes to fit the length of the tank. You'll need to rake in both directions to create the basic get gel pattern upon which most other patterns are based, and a long rake can do double duty. Since its teeth are spaced wide apart, it can straddle the wall of the tank and hang out over the side while you rake up and down the length of the tank.

In addition, tools should feel comfortable in your hands and be light enough so that they're not tiring to use. They should be made of materials that won't give you splinters or rust when wet.

Use your imagination and the materials at hand. If there's a piece of rigid-foam packing left over from the package that came in the morning mail, cut it the proper length and stick a row of straight pins down one side of it; you've got a marbling comb. There are as many homemade solutions as there are marblers.

RAKES

1. Cut a piece of corrugated cardboard an inch or two wide (2.5 to 5 cm.) and slightly shorter than the length of your tray. (Length and width refer to the tank's inside dimensions.) Cut the strip perpendicular to the corrugations, or ridges, so that its long edges contain handy little pre-measured holes all the same size and distance apart. Get some curler picks—they're plastic, usually pink, and have been keeping women awake at night for years—and insert them into the holes at regular intervals. Seal the rake with non-water-soluble glue (hot glue is perfect) or strapping tape or both. Let dry.

2. Cut a strip of wood one inch wide (2.5 cm.) and slightly shorter than the length of the tray. Lay the wood flat, and draw a line down the center of it. Along that line, measure and mark off regular intervals (however far apart you want the teeth to be). Drill holes through the wood at the marks. Insert rust-proof nails through the holes, and secure them with a little waterproof glue. Coat the wood with a protective coating, such as polyurethane.

Hint: Before drilling, make sure the nails and the drill bit are about the same size.

COMBS

1. Cut a piece of balsa wood one inch wide (2.5 cm.) and slightly shorter than the inside width of the tray. Stick stainless steel straight pins into one long edge at regular intervals. Secure the pins with waterproof glue. For more strength, cover each side of the wood with strapping tape, overlapped at the ends.

Make sure to use pins with substantial heads. You'll need something relatively comfortable to push against, and the heads will be below the surface, out of the way, when you marble. (The shafts of the pins will move the paint.)

2. Cut two strips of wood one to two inches wide (2.5 to 5 cm.) and slightly shorter than the width of the tank. Cover one side of a strip with waterproof glue, and place straight pins or T-pins at regular intervals. (It helps to place the other wood strip alongside, so that it can prop up the points of the pins while you're gluing.) Let dry. Apply a second coat of glue, and attach the other piece of wood. Let dry. Brush on a protective coating such as polyurethane, or cover the wood with strapping tape.

BOUQUET COMB

To make the traditional peacock and bouquet patterns (see pages 52 and 62), you'll need a bouquet comb, which has two rows of alternating teeth.

Cut a strip of wood two inches wide (5 cm.) and as long as the inside width of the tank. Draw two lines down its length, each a half-inch in from an edge. Mark off two-inch (5 cm.) intervals along one line. Then mark off two-inch intervals along the second line, locating each mark halfway between the marks on the first line. Drill holes at the marks, and insert nails. Glue the nails in place, and cover the wood with a waterproof coating, such as polyurethane.

THE SIZE

Whether you're marbling paper or fabric, the paints must float on a "size," or "bath"—water that has been thickened to a consistency reminiscent of gelatin that's just beginning to set. (Among younger marblers, size is known admiringly as "slime.")

■

The thicker the stylus, the more it will "drag" the paint across the surface. The same rule applies to the tines of a rake and the teeth of a comb—the thicker they are, the more action there will be on the surface. (How much you want depends on the effect you're aiming for. A fine, detailed pattern needs thinner teeth.)

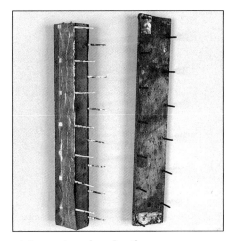

A bouquet comb makes the traditional bouquet and peacock patterns.

PAPER

For marbling paper, the sizing agent is carragheen moss, a cold-water seaweed commonly known as "Irish moss." When this seaweed is boiled, an insulating gum that coats it dissolves, thickening the surrounding liquid. For years marblers collected handfuls of seaweed, dried it, boiled it, strained it in a colander, and re-strained it through muslin.

Mercifully, an extract of Irish moss is now available in powdered form. Known as carrageenan, it requires only a brief turn in the blender. Although carrageenan isn't sold on every street corner, it is readily available from marbling suppliers and in some health food stores. It's not as alien as it may sound. Food manufacturers have used it for years to stabilize ice cream, puddings, and yogurt. In fact, some marbling suppliers obtain their carrageenan from food companies and accurately describe it as "food grade."

Making carrageenan size. The basic proportions are two tablespoons of carrageenan for each gallon of water.

To make one gallon of size, fill a blender three-quarters full with tepid water, and turn it on. Add one tablespoon of carrageenan, and blend for 60 seconds. Expect the mixture to be foamy, but make sure it's smooth; if lumps remain, they will leave their imprint on the marbled paper. Pour the mixture into a large bucket.

Blend the second tablespoon of carrageenan with a blenderful of water, and add that to the bucket. Add enough water to the bucket to equal one gallon of size, and stir.

To make more than one gallon, just increase the ingredients as much as necessary, keeping the same proportions. Blend all the carrageenan a tablespoon at a time, and then add water to the total volume required.

A rake created from a lightweight piece of wood and some hair-curler picks.

Fill the marbling tray, and allow the size to age for about 12 hours. If you work on an immature size, the marbled lines will have rough edges, if indeed the paints agree to form any pattern at all. Moreover, fresh size is full of air bubbles, which will leave naked white specks on the marbled paper.

TIPS AND ADVICE

Water quality. Because water is so central to marbling—it's in the size, the mordant, and the paint—its quality is critical. Water should be soft; the minerals in hard water may upset the process. Rainwater is good, unless acid rain is acute in your area.

If your first marbling attempts fail utterly, your water is the prime suspect. Try using distilled water. While it may be too expensive as a permanent solution for the size, at least you've isolated the problem. Frequently a neighbor with better water will donate size-making water in exchange for an occasional marbled T-shirt.

Contamination. Make sure that your tools—blender, spoon, and bucket—are free of food and soap residues before making the size. While the carrageenan won't hurt your food, the food will spoil the carrageenan.

Consistency. This recipe is a guideline, not a prescription; you may well prefer a thicker or thinner size. (The more carrageenan, the thicker the size.) When you adjust the size, you'll also need to adjust the paint: a thinner size requires thinner paints.

Volume. How much size to make at one time depends on several factors. The marbling tray should be filled to a depth of one to two inches (2.5 to 5 cm.), so you'll need to make at least that much. After that, it's a matter of how much marbling you plan to do in how short a time.

Carrageenan size will spoil—it is, after all, essentially a marine vegetable broth—and it will spoil faster in hot weather, certainly within a few days. Spoilage is not hard to detect. For one thing, the size will lose its viscosity and thin out. For another, your entire house will begin to smell as if the Irish Sea is lapping at the front steps.

FABRIC

Fabric can be marbled on carrageenan size, and many well-known marblers do just that, citing the predictability of the medium and the precise patterns it makes possible. But carrageenan has some disadvantages for fabric. Most notably, the acrylic paints used on fabric contaminate carrageenan very quickly. A bath may yield as little as a day's marbling before paint dropped on the surface forms jagged splotches, rather than the round, smooth-edged stones that every marbler wants. If skimming the surface doesn't work, then the entire bath is contaminated and must be discarded. Another sign of contamination is that the size thins out.

A longer-lasting size, and the choice of many fabric marblers, is methyl cellulose, a wood pulp extract. Like carrageenan, "methyl cel" is an organic product. In fact, some gardeners use it around the base of their plants to hold moisture in the roots.

Making methyl cellulose size. To make fabric size, stir four table-spoons of methyl cellulose into one gallon of warm water. Add two tablespoons of clear ammonia, and stir until the mixture looks clear. Then add two teaspoons of white vinegar, and stir. Pour into the marbling tray, and let stand for about 12 hours.

When methyl cellulose is stirred into warm water, the powder disperses but does not dissolve. At this stage, it is only in suspension. For the powder to dissolve, the water must be alkaline—hence the addition of ammonia, an alkaline compound. The acid vinegar brings the size back to neutral, which is where it should be for marbling.

If you live in an area with alkaline water—for example, the American Southwest—add 2 teaspoons of white

MORDANT

Paper, fabric, wood, or clay—if it is to be marbled, it must first be mordanted, a concept familiar to weavers who dye their own yarns and sewers who dye their own cloth. A mordant is a chemical that combines with a dye to form an insoluble compound, thus fixing a color permanently.

For marblers, the mordant is aluminum, or "alum," available in three different crystalline salts: aluminum sulfate, potassium aluminum sulfate, and ammonium aluminum sulfate. The alum is dissolved in water and applied to the paper or fabric.

Any of the alums will do; highly competent marblers swear by all three. Those craftspeople with no strong preference use whatever is locally available (if anything is), for the sake of convenience and to avoid shipping charges. Potassium aluminum sulfate is usually obtainable wherever dyeing supplies are sold. If there is no alum around town, it is readily available from mail-order suppliers. Some marblers even resort to pickling alum in a bind.

With all alums, the general rule is to use just enough and no more. If the alum solution is too weak, the paint will not bond well to the surface, and the color will be pale, uneven, and streaked.

On the other hand, if the solution is too strong, a thick layer of alum will build up on the surface of the paper or cloth. During marbling, the paint will adhere to this crust of alum rather than to the fiber, and both alum and paint will slough off during rinsing, leaving a pale splotch behind.

Moreover, alum is an acid compound. The stronger the solution, the more acidic the paper or fabric becomes and thus the shorter its life span will be. Ask any librarian about the priceless old books that are crumbling into confetti because they were printed on acid paper. The trick is to discover the weakest solution that will do the job.

PAPER

Solution. Add 1-1/4 cups alum to a gallon of hot water (300 ml. to 3.8 liters), and stir until dissolved. Allow solution to cool to room temperature before applying, to save wear and tear on the paper.

Application. Pour the alum solution into a shallow tray that's large enough to hold the paper. (The marbling tray will serve, as long as it's carefully washed between aluming and marbling.) Lay a sheet of paper on the surface. Make sure that the entire sheet is dampened; any areas that receive no alum will likewise retain no paint. Lift the paper off the tray, and hang it on an ordinary clothesline with even-more-ordinary clothespins. Decide which direction the mordanted side will face—you'll mordant only one side, and when the paper is dry you won't be able to tell which side is which—and hang all pieces of paper facing the same way. (Or mark the treated side.)

After the paper is dry, it must be pressed. Stack the sheets, again facing in the same direction. (If they lie mordanted-side-down, they'll be facing the right way when it's time to marble.) Cover the stack with a board or piece of hardboard, and place a heavy weight on top—say, an encyclopedia, Volume "M," or a cement block.

TIPS AND ADVICE

Alternative aluming. Marblers apply alum in a variety of ways. A more traditional way to mordant paper is with a sponge. For this approach, pour the alum solution into a spray bottle, and mist it on the paper. Then wipe the paper with a damp sponge, using overlapping

vinegar to the water before adding the methyl cel, to bring the water to neutral. (The powder will disperse only in a neutral liquid, and if it doesn't disperse first, it won't dissolve well.) Then proceed with the methyl cel, the ammonia, and more vinegar. No detective work is required to determine whether your water is alkaline. If it is, you've dealt with other consequences before you ever started marbling.

■

Once fabric is mordanted, it must be marbled within a week. Otherwise, it will rot, especially if it's silk. If something intervenes between aluming and marbling, wash and dry the fabric, then mordant it again when you're ready to marble.

■

Mordant can weaken as it sits. If it gets cold, then warm, then cold, the aluminum will recrystallize and fall to the bottom, leaving a weakened solution. Reheating will redissolve the alum.

■

Like different papers, individual fabrics can vary in the amount of alum they need. If you're working with a particularly expensive or valued piece of cloth, you might want to test a small scrap, starting with a weak solution and adding alum until you get a good result.

■

strokes and distributing the alum evenly over the entire surface.

Alternatively, apply the mordant directly with the sponge. Dip it in the solution and ring it out—it should be just damp—and spread mordant directly on the paper, using vertical, overlapping strokes, then horizontal ones, again trying for an even application. The paper should be damp, not shiny or saturated.

Aluming in a tray is the most convenient method, and the one most likely to produce an evenly alumned piece of paper. (You may use that statement to start arguments with other marblers almost at will.) With the sponge method, it is difficult to get an even application of alum, which means that some areas of the marbled paper will be paler than others. It's also difficult to avoid "swipe marks"—areas where the strokes overlapped and left tracks that will appear as if by magic in the marbled print.

Damp or dry. Sponge-mordanted paper can be marbled after it's dried, as described above, or while it's still damp. Damp marbling is a hassle—it requires constantly alternating between mordanting and marbling, because the paper has to be marbled before it dries out, say within 30 minutes. Devotees of damp marbling say the advantages are worth the extra effort—that the chemical bond of alum and paint is stronger, leaving the marbled papers less apt to smudge. They also maintain that damp paper is easier to lay on the tray.

We suggest that you start out by mordanting in a tray, and that you marble dry paper. After that, experimentation is the order of the day.

Protection. Rubber gloves are strongly recommended when mixing or applying any of the alums. Aluminum is absorbed through the skin, and the body apparently has no way to get rid of it. Among health professionals it is widely suspected that various health problems are linked to high levels of aluminum.

Strength. The alum solution suggested above will work for most papers most of the time, but different types of paper and different types of alum may require different strengths. At least one expert has made an excellent case for simple aluminum sulfate as the alum that functions well in the weakest solution, but the question is not definitively settled. It's a good area for individual experimentation, always aiming for the weakest solution possible.

Weather. Paper that's mordanted on a rainy day will dry evenly and smooth.

FABRIC

Before fabric is mordanted, it must be washed and dried to remove whatever sizing the manufacturer has added. Otherwise, neither alum nor paint will adhere to the fiber. (If the fabric isn't washable—that is, if it can't get wet—then it can't be marbled.)

Solution. Add 1/2 cup alum to a gallon of hot water (100 ml. to 3.8

liters) and stir until dissolved. Let the solution sit until it's room temperature.

Application. Pour the mordant into a bucket and immerse the fabric in it, making sure all of the material is covered.

Fabrics vary in the length of time they need to soak. Silk scarves require as little as 15 minutes, cotton broadcloth half an hour, a heavy sweatshirt a full hour.

Squeeze out the excess solution, and dry the fabric. Although cotton can be line-dried, it works very well in a dryer; the tumbling and constant heat prevent the streaking that can result from uneven drying.

Silk must be line-dried. For one thing, it shrinks in a dryer. For another, a clothes dryer leaches alum from silk, leaving an under-alumed piece of fabric that will be pale when it's marbled. Make sure that the silk doesn't fold back on itself while it's hanging to dry. Where it is doubled it will be over-alumed, resulting in an unevenly colored garment.

When the fabric is dry, press it with an iron, so that it is wrinkle-free for marbling.

PAINTS

If you'd like to test a marbler's reflexes, take a rake that's been used for marbling fabric and hold it threateningly above a tank that's all prepared for paper marbling. That catlike speed and that viselike grip on your wrist resulted from the chemical incompatibility of paints used for fabric and those used for paper.

PAPER

To mix paints for marbling paper, you'll need three ingredients: pigment, water, and ox gall. (Yes, ox gall.)

Pigments. The best pigments—certainly the easiest ones to use—are water-base paints ground specifically for marbling, available from a number of suppliers. Other options are some brands of gouaches and watercolors. Since these are touchier to work with and less likely to yield happy results, they are not recommended for beginners.

Water. Soft water is fine for diluting paints; distilled water is excellent.

Ox gall. The last ingredient is accurately named—it really is bile from the gall bladder of a cow—and it's just about as appetizing as it sounds. Art supply stores do stock a white, purified, inoffensive ox gall but, alas, it's too weak for your purposes. You need the disgusting green liquid that only a marbling supplier is willing to stock.

Ox gall does two things. First, it is a "surfactant," a surface-active ingredient that enables the paint to resist the surface tension of the

A collection of water-base marbling paints, complete with whisks.

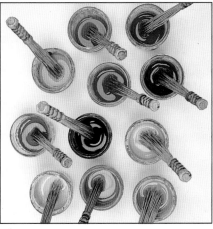

bath and thus to float. (Surface tension, you may recall, is the desire of molecules below the surface of a liquid to drag the surface molecules down to their level.) Second, the fatty ox gall surrounds each droplet of paint so that it can't blend with a second color to form a third. Each color remains distinct, allowing for crisp, multicolored patterns.

Mixing the paints. First, prepare a pan of size on which to test the paints. An eight-inch by eight-inch (20 by 20 cm.) baking pan should provide enough surface tension to mimic a normal-size bath and will allow you to test the paints without dirtying the bath. You'll also need a small container for each color—a jelly jar, for example, or a plastic cup.

Start with a small amount of paint—say, two or three tablespoons. Add water until the paint is the consistency of whole milk. How much water that will be varies wildly among suppliers and even among colors from the same supplier. Five-to-one paint-to-water may work for one supplier; two-to-one water to paint for another. Read the supplier's catalog, phone if necessary, and experiment.

To the diluted paint add one drop of ox gall. Skim the pan, and sprinkle a few drops of paint on the surface. If the paint sinks, skim the surface, add another drop of gall to the paint, and try again.

Keep adding gall drop by drop until the paint floats and spreads out into a circle anywhere from a half inch to two inches in diameter (13 mm. to 5 cm.). If you add too much and the paint spreads too far, add some paint and test again.

Repeat the process with each color you plan to use. When they all behave admirably alone, test them together, to see if they all float and spread as they should when they share the same surface.

The more ox gall that is added to the paint, the better it floats and the wider it spreads across the surface of the bath—in other words, the bigger the stone. Corollary: The more ox gall, the paler the color.

TIPS AND ADVICE

Tools. It's wise to test the paint with the same tool you plan to marble with. If you're going to use a whisk, test with a whisk. The tiny droplets that flick off a piece of broom corn will float with less gall than will the larger, heavier drops from an eye dropper. If you test with one implement and marble with another, you may find that your paints are improperly adjusted.

Skimming. It's important to skim the surface of the bath every time you test the paint. The skin that begins to form within seconds will prevent the paint from spreading properly, and will seduce you into adding more gall than you need.

Size. How big you want your stones to be is a matter of personal preference. As a starting point, try for a circle between a quarter and a half dollar.

Stirring. Marbling watercolors are suspensions, not solutions; they

Acrylic fabric paints in narrow-tipped plastic bottles.

must be stirred constantly. If you're using a lot of colors, it could take you an hour to stir the paints before a marbling session. As you work, stir each color before you lay it down.

Whisks. Each jar of paint requires its own whisk.

Ox gall. A popular piece of marbling lore is that each color laid needs more ox gall than the one previous to it, if all are to spread properly.

The reasoning is this: The first color needs only to overcome the surface tension of the bath. The second color must overcome the surface tension and push aside the first color in order to spread; thus, it needs more spreading power than the first if it is to cover equal territory. And so on for colors, three, four, and five.

While the chemistry is correct, the rule presumes, first, that you know what colors you plan to use and the order in which you intend to use them; and, second, that you want them to spread in equal amounts.

Intensity. If you don't vary the paints' spreading power, the first color laid becomes the most compressed—all subsequent colors will force it into narrow veins—and thus will be intense. Look at the "Stones" pattern on page 44. The first color, an indigo blue, was compressed until it appears almost black. If you plan to use black, try it as a first color, compressed into an ebony outline of other hues. Used as a later color, it will diffuse into gray.

Color dominance. The last color laid will be the most prominent one in the pattern, unless the amounts used vary enormously.

FABRIC

The whole issue of paint is simpler for fabric than for paper. There's no need to order specially made paints. You need only the acrylic fabric paints widely available in craft shops. There are a number of brands, and they come in a marvelous array of colors. Experiment until you find the brand you prefer—or even the colors in each brand (although different brands don't always mix comfortably with each other). Buy small jars to start.

What will not work are fabric dyes. Rather than floating on the surface of the size, they obligingly dissolve in it, leaving you with a colorful bath but with no prospect of marbling.

Unlike watercolors for paper, most fabric paints require no surfactant in order to float and spread into proper stones. Additives in the paints produce that effect. They simply have to be thinned with water. Some brands do work better with the addition of a little Photo-Flo, available at photo-supply stores. If you've added so much water that the color is turning pale and the paint still refuses to float, try the Photo-Flo.

How much water paints need varies from brand to brand. Even within the same line, colors have different personalities and demand

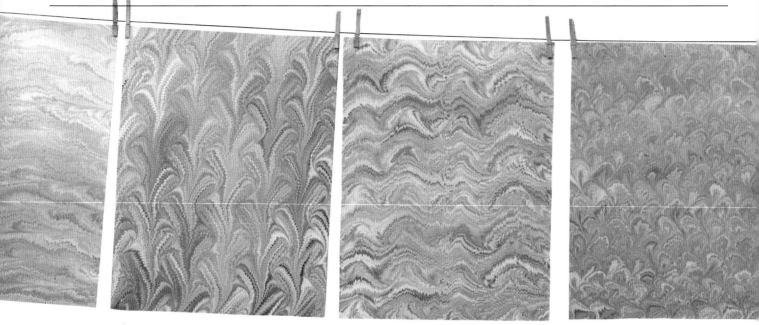

differing amounts before they'll float and spread.

Usually paints work best when they're the consistency of whole milk or light cream. For many colors this means equal amounts of water and paint, or about two parts water to one part paint.

Pour some size into a small pan (for example, an eight-inch by eight-inch baking pan), and test the paints. Pour a little pigment into a small container—say, a plastic bottle with a pointed cap—and add water, a little at a time, until the paint floats when dropped on the surface and forms a stone the size you like. If the center of the stone falls, add more water. If the stone spreads too much, add more paint. After each color works properly, test several colors at the same time.

TIPS AND ADVICE

Stones. Many marblers prefer larger stones for fabric than for paper—say, three or four inches (7.5 to 10 cm.).

Water. Fabric paints last longer if they're diluted with distilled water. When they're through lasting, they break up and become grainy. Some colors of some brands are permanently grainy, no matter what you do. That's just the way they are.

Stirring. Acrylics don't require the constant stirring that watercolors do. Still, an occasional shake does them a world of good.

Retesting. Before each marbling session, test each color on the bath or on a separate pan of size the same temperature as your bath. If, as a group, the colors refuse to spread, the size may be too cold or too thick. If the colors spread into dinner plates, the size may be warm, too thin, too young, or too old.

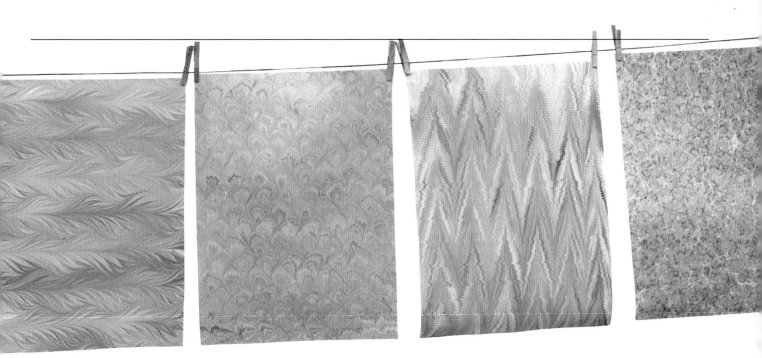

MATERIAL

Of the almost limitless papers and fabrics available, some accept marbling better than others.

PAPER

Papers that marble well meet several criteria. First, they have wet strength. Paper has to be strong enough to get wet twice—once when it's mordanted and once when it's marbled. Moreover, it must be able to support its own weight when it's lifted wet from the tank (twice) and when it's hung to dry. If alum is applied with a sponge, the paper must withstand that abrasion.

Second, the paper must be relatively flexible. If it's so stiff that it won't bend easily and smoothly, you won't be able to lay it down on the size in one fluid motion. The results will be air bubbles, hesitation marks, and a distorted pattern.

Third, the paper must be willing to take the color.

Art papers for charcoaling (use the smoother side), for drawing, or for pastels work extremely well, but they tend to be expensive. Printing papers of between 65 and 75 pound text weight are more affordable and produce excellent results. There are just a few pitfalls.

If the paper is too slick, it will absorb neither the alum nor the color. Paint slides right off paper that's calendared or super-shiny. Fluorescent papers don't work well either—they usually have names like

PAPER

Marbling on colored paper can produce hues of remarkable depth and richness. (Besides, flaws don't show up as clearly.) Just keep in mind that the color of the paper affects all the paints that are put on it. If you marble on blue paper, you're adding a little bit of blue to every pigment you use.

■

The wisest course is to buy paper in the smallest amounts possible until you find the kind you're happy with, and then buy it in quantity. (This assumes it's from the same batch; paper varies from batch to batch, even the same type from the same manufacturer.)

■

Even when you find a paper that works, keep experimenting with different papers. Manufacturers will supply sample books that provide all sorts of inspiration. (See "Paper Distributors" in the telephone directory.)

"bright white" or "fluorescent white." If the paper has been treated with excessive sizing, it will repel the color, and if it has too coarse a weave, the patterns will be fuzzy and indistinct. Also problematic are construction paper (it bleeds and later fades), newsprint (it falls apart), and sketch pad paper (it accepts color unevenly). Avoid papers that "cockle" (wrinkle and buckle) badly when they're wet. (You won't know that until you use it, of course, but at least you can avoid it a second time.)

FABRIC

A variety of fabrics will accept marbling. Natural fibers take the color best; most "pure" polyesters don't do well, although there's the occasional exception. Smooth fabrics produce colors that are especially vibrant.

Because fabric can represent a considerable outlay, it's worthwhile to buy a small piece and test it before investing in any appreciable yardage. And because marbling fabric is a relatively new craft, it makes sense to experiment with fabrics that no one has recommended. All these work well:

Cotton	Silk blends
Pima cotton	Chenille
Some cotton-poly blends	Rayon
Silk	Linen

CHECKLIST OF MATERIALS FOR MARBLING PAPER

SIZE:
Carrageenan
Blender
5-gallon bucket for mixing size
Long-handled spoon for stirring
Tablespoon

MORDANT:
Alum
Bucket or plastic jug for mixing alum
Tray or sponge for application
1 sheet of plywood or hardboard, slightly larger than papers to be marbled, for pressing them flat after aluming
Rubber gloves

COLOR   Paint containers, such as small jars
Marbling paints
Ox gall and eye dropper
Applicators: whisks, brushes, eye droppers
Small flat pan for testing colors

MARBLING: Tray
Pattern-making tools
Paper

RINSING AND DRYING:
Rinse board
Faucet and sink, or plastic jug and bucket
Clothesline
Clothespins

CHECKLIST OF MATERIALS FOR MARBLING FABRIC

SIZE: Methyl cellulose
Ammonia
Vinegar
Long-handled spoon for stirring

MORDANT: Alum
5-gallon bucket for mixing alum and soaking fabric
Rubber gloves

COLOR: Fabric paints
Applicators: plastic narrow-tipped bottles, eye droppers, brushes

MARBLING: Tray
Pattern-making tools
Fabric

RINSING AND DRYING:
Sink and faucet, or 2 or 3 five-gallon buckets
Clothesline
Clothespins

■

Keep a written record of what papers you test (perhaps even samples) and how they work. You think you'll remember, but you won't.

■

FABRIC

You can often tell whether a cotton-poly blend will marble well without buying a square inch. Pull an end thread. If it looks like cotton, the fabric will probably work. If it tufts up into a "poly puff," marbling will be pale; the paint won't adhere well to the fabric.

■

Like tinted paper, colored fabric is exciting to work with, yielding rich and diverse colors. Keep in mind that the color of the fabric will bleed through the paint, creating an optical blend. When mixing two hues (paint and fabric), cast an assessing eye at both, and try to predict what you will get if you use that sunny yellow paint on that royal blue silk. (Hint: Green.)

MARBLING STEP BY STEP

After a few experimental marblings, the steps in the process become second nature. Then it's a matter of refining specific techniques—for example, laying the paper or fabric on the surface of the tray in one smooth, rhythmic motion.

PREPARATION

1. Make the size, and let it sit for 12 hours.

2. Mordant the paper or fabric, and let it dry. Iron fabric; wrinkles will leave white lines in the marbling.

3. Arrange the work area.

You'll need good light, either natural or artificial, and a table or counter that's a comfortable working height and large enough to hold tray, paints, tools, and three-inch-wide strips (7.5 cm.) of newspaper as

A marbler lays the paint (1-3), makes the pattern (4-8), lays the paper (9-10), lifts the marbled paper (11), and rinses it off (12).

32

long as the tray is wide. Running water is convenient but not essential.

There are two other requirements. Since the size and paints should be the same temperature during marbling, it's helpful if you can leave everything set up in the same area for some time beforehand. Second, if the work space is too cold (say, below 60°) or too hot (above 80°) for your comfort, the marbling may also be affected. If the work area is humid, so much the better; high humidity helps keep dust under control.

Cover the floor with newspaper or a drop cloth—under the table, the rinse area, and the clothesline. All these areas will get wet and slippery from the size. Also cover the work table with newsprint, as it will get wet and paint-spattered.

Position the tray so that you can stand at one short end. Have the paints close to the tray, with the patterning tools in between, so you don't knock over the paints with the tools. The paper or fabric should be out of splatter range but within easy reach. (Once you've got the

design you want, it should be printed immediately; left to sit on the surface, it will start to disintegrate.) Put a waste basket next to the table.

Set up the rinse area. For paper, you need a rinse board that's larger than the paper, to support the marbled paper while it's being rinsed. You'll also need either a sink with running water, or something to pour clean water from (say, a plastic jug) and something to catch the water that runs off the paper (a bucket or dishpan big enough to set the rinse board in).

For fabric, you'll need either a sink with running water, or a five-gallon bucket of water.

Hang up a clothesline, and keep clothespins handy nearby.

4. Wear old clothes or an apron you don't mind staining; you're going to get wet and paint-smeared.

PAPER

1. Mix and test the paints.

2. Skim the size.

Drag one of the newspaper strips across the surface of the bath, thus breaking up the surface skin and removing air bubbles and any paint left over from a previous print. Discard the paper.

Paint that has sunk to the bottom or remains suspended in the bath will not affect the print; you'll be working only on the surface. Residues become a problem when the bath or the bottom is so murky that you can't tell what's on the surface and what is below.

3. Apply the colors.

A *whisk* is an efficient tool that allows you to quickly cover the tray with small, controllable drops of color. It is probably the most widely used

THE GOOD, THE BAD, AND THE UGLY

Good marbling and pretty marbling are not always identical. A technically competent piece can be just plain ugly—colors that "should" have worked together didn't, at least not with that pattern. Likewise, bad marbling can be pleasing, like an ill-proportioned puppy that's irresistible. What ultimately matters is what you like.

Still, as you experiment, and as you survey all the marbled goods for sale, it's useful to have some criteria for spotting the good stuff.

1. Is the pattern clear, rather than confused? (For that matter, is there a pattern?) Even free-form marbling should hang together, should look as if the marbler had something in mind.

2. Are the lines sharp and clear, rather than fuzzy and wobbling?

3. Are the blemishes minimal? Dust spots and air bubbles are part of the craft, but good craftspeople keep them at a minimum. Certainly the flaws should not be the most attention-getting part of the piece.

4. Are the color combinations interesting or trite? Are those same three hues keeping

applicator for paper.

Stir the first color you plan to use vigorously with its whisk. Lift the whisk out of the color and tap it gently against the rim, to get rid of excess color. Hold the whisk about a foot above the bath and tap it against the forefinger of your other hand, moving your hands over the bath until the entire surface has some paint. Repeat if you want more of the same color.

Then move to the second color, the third, and so on until the surface is well covered.

An *eye dropper* is a very precise applicator—it allows you to put a single drop of color exactly where you want it. For example, you can drop stones exactly in the center of each other, for the makings of some very interesting patterns, especially for the stylus.

On the other hand, an eye dropper is very slow—you'll have to cover the surface of the tank literally drop by drop.

To use the dropper, stir the color and fill the dropper with paint. Hold the eye dropper close above the surface, and release a drop of paint. Don't let up on the pressure; if air is sucked back up the tube between drops, subsequent stones will have air bubbles.

4. Manipulate the paints.

You can rake and comb at will or make any of the traditional patterns explained in the glossary (see page 42).

5. Lay the paper.

Take a sheet from the alumed stack and hold it in both hands by diagonal corners, alumed side down. Starting at one corner, roll the paper onto the surface in one continuous motion. If the paper fails to make contact with the surface because of an air pocket, try to tap it down.

company all over town?

5. Is there a feeling of abundance, a sense of possibility? After gazing at the surface for a few minutes, do you realize that you saw everything there was to see in the first three seconds—or did you discover the lavender only at fifth glance?

6. Good marbling often surprises. If your first thought is, "I would never have thought of combining those exact colors," you may be on to something. (If your second thought is, "And now I know why," maybe not.)

7. Finally, by some indefinable alchemy, do all the elements combine to form a whole—a creation, a presence—so that those colors and that pattern seem, for the moment, inseparable? If they do—and if you like it—you've got good marbling.

As soon as all parts of the paper have been wetted by the paint, peel off the paper and carry it to the rinse board.

Be careful not to touch the wet print except by the corners, or the paint will smear.

6. Rinse the paper.

Lay the paper (paint side up) on the board, and rinse it with cool water, to remove any size. Hang the marbled sheet from the clothesline to dry.

FABRIC

A marbler skims the size (1), lays the paint (2-3), makes the pattern (4-9), lays the fabric (10), lifts it off (11), and rinses it.

1. Mix and test the paints.

2. Skim the size with the strips of newspaper.

3. Apply the colors, with whisks, snout-tipped plastic bottles, or eye droppers.

4. Manipulate the paints, either working free-style or making one of the traditional patterns in the glossary (page 42).

5. Lay the fabric, and leave it on the surface for about a minute.

If you can find a helper, each of you can take two corners of the fabric. Position the cloth over the tank, and let it droop in the middle. Lay it "belly first" on the surface, so that the center of the fabric makes contact first; then allow it to droop smoothly and evenly out to the edges. Try to hold the fabric with equal tension on all four sides, or air may be trapped along one edge, leaving a long white streak.

To work alone, make a couple of handles for the fabric, so that you can control it. You'll need two wooden skewers (the kind used for shish-kabob) or two small dowels (an eighth of an inch or a quarter of an inch in diameter, or 3 to 6 mm.) and some straight pins.

Tape a straight pin to each end of both sticks, needle end pointing out. Attach the sticks across the ends of the fabric from selvage to selvage, with the pin point catching the selvage.

6. Rinse the fabric.

Peel fabric off the size, being careful not to touch it except at the corners. Otherwise, the paint may smear.

If you have a sink handy, extend the fabric under the faucet and rinse in cool water. If not, place it in a large bucket of clean water.

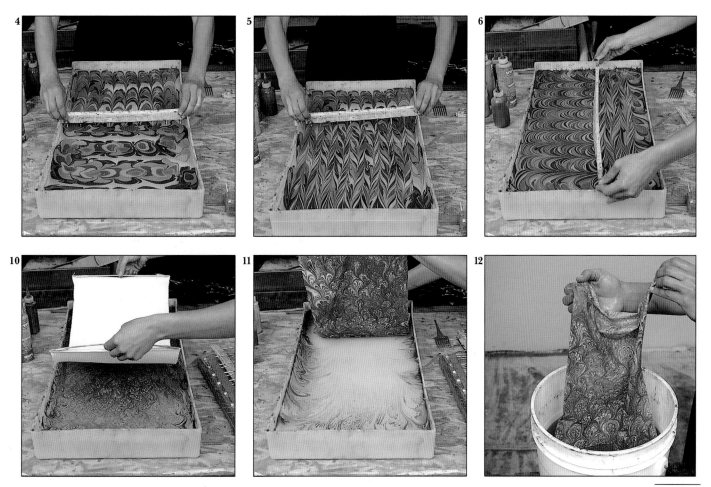

Design.
Marbling began as a means of decorating paper. Books, manuscripts, and prints are relatively small and static; the reader holds them close and lingers over them. Thus, patterns were appropriately small and intricate, and colors often subdued.
The rules have changed, however. Marbled paper is now used for everything from waste baskets to Christmas cards.
And fabric is even more different. It is frequently seen from a distance, often as it moves. Thus small, complex patterns may be less effective than large, open ones. Moreover, if the fabric itself is interesting, sections of it can be left bare of paint, so that the weave shows through. When selecting colors

7. Hang the fabric to dry.

After it's dry, let it sit for two days to a week to cure. Then heat-set the paint by tumbling the cloth in a hot dryer for 20 minutes, or iron the fabric on the wrong side for about three minutes. (Check the label of the fabric paint for recommended times.)

CLEAN-UP

Since the marbling process can be contaminated, clean-up is important and not especially awful. Avoid soap; any residues will contaminate the next session.

If the bath is too dirty for further use, throw it out and scrub the tray with warm water. If there's more marbling left in this batch, cover as a protection against dust.

Cover leftover paints. Hold whisks under running water until it runs clear, and rinse off patterning tools. Pick up all those newspapers and throw them away.

COLOR

Color is the soul of marbling. Pattern, line, and rhythm may be important, but it's color that draws us across the room to run a marbled scarf through our fingers.

Traditional color theory provides some useful concepts for analyzing what we see, and for understanding why some of our combinations work and others don't.

THE DIMENSIONS OF COLOR

Hue. A color's common name—red, yellow, blue—is its hue. Every color falls within a hue category.

Value. Value refers to a color's relative lightness or darkness—where it falls on the scale from white to black. In a black-and-white photograph, hues are invisible; values are visible as various shades of gray. Yellow is high in value (closer to the white end of the scale); violet is low in value (closer to black).

A *tint* results when white is added to a color—for example, pink is a tint of red. Adding black to a color produces a *shade*. Obviously, a tint is higher in value than a shade.

Intensity. The third dimension of color, intensity, describes the difference between a brilliant red and a dull red. Both are the same hue, but their brightness varies.

COLOR HARMONIES

Most craft stores stock color wheels, larger and more detailed versions of the one on the next page. They are enormously helpful in stimulating a marbler's creativity with color.

Monochromatic. A monochromatic color plan uses a single hue in various values and intensities. A pale blue scarf marbled with royal blue and deep indigo is a monochromatic harmony.

Analogous. Analogous harmony involves two or three hues from one segment of the color circle—for example, blue and violet, orange and yellow, red and violet. Because an analogous color scheme is taken from one side of the hue circle, it has a prevailing temperature. For example, a design worked in yellow and orange is warm; one worked in blue and green is cool.

Direct complements. Two hues are direct complements if they are directly opposite each other on the hue circle. For example, yellow and violet are direct complements; so are blue-green and red-orange, and blue-violet and yellow-orange.

Direct complements provide the strongest color contrasts, and frequently work better as tints or shades than as pure colors.

Triadic harmonies. Imagine a triangle placed over a hue circle, with its three points touching three hues; the result is a triadic harmony. An equilateral triangle would touch three hues equidistant from each other—for example, violet, green, and orange; or red, blue, and yellow. An isosceles triangle would produce split harmonies—for example, yellow, red violet, and blue violet. (Split complements are the two hues on either side of the direct complement.) Split complements often provide subtler, less strident harmonies than direct complements.

and patterns for paper or fabric, it helps to consider intended use. Then the scale of the pattern can be matched to the size of the item. For example, an evening bag can carry off a smaller pattern than a pillow case. (Bed sheets would be nice, but consider the tray.) Baby rompers (page 84) require a daintier pattern than a tablecloth (page 92), unless you want to mesmerize guests during dinner. Scale is less important in paper marbling, because size varies less. Still, intended use matters. A desk set (page 108) should not be marbled in vibrant colors that assault hardworking eyes, but Christmas cards (page 112) can be as lively as the season.

GLITCHES

When marbling works, it works very, very well. When it fails, it is horrid.

Because the same problem may result from any number of causes—even opposite causes—finding the source of the trouble, much less a solution, can be difficult. (The patience of marblers is legendary.)

The best approach is to change one variable at a time. Adjust the paints; if that doesn't work, adjust the size; if that doesn't work, you might consider taking up embroidery, which also has some interesting colors and patterns to recommend it.

A color wheel is invaluable in planning color harmonies.

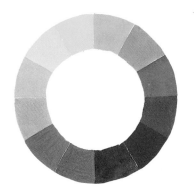

Problem: The paint sinks when dropped on the size.
  Cause: The size is too thick, or the paint doesn't have enough ox gall (watercolors) or enough water (acrylics).
Solution: Add water to the size, or adjust the paint.

Problem: The paint spreads too much when dropped on the size.
  Cause: The size is too thin, too old, or too warm; or the paint contains too much ox gall (watercolors) or too much water (acrylics).
Solution: Make new size, or adjust the paint.

Problem: When paint is dropped on the size, the stone spreads and then contracts.
  Cause: The size is too cold.
Solution: Add warm water to the size; or, if that will make it too thin, make some warm size and add it to the tray.

Problem: Paint dropped on the size forms jagged blotches rather than smooth stones.
  Cause: A skin has formed on the surface.
Solution: Skim the bath.

Problem: The marbled surface is sprinkled with small white dots.
  Cause: Dust settled on the surface of the bath.
Solution: Re-skim the surface, and keep the tank covered when not in use. If all else fails, clean the work area.

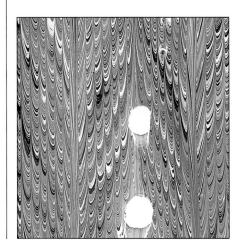

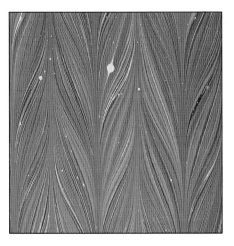

Problem: There is a large white blob on the paper or fabric where the color didn't take.
Cause: An air bubble on the surface of the size held the paper or fabric up off the paint.
Solution: Skim surface carefully, and lay the paper or fabric down in one smooth, continuous motion, without trapping air between the item being marbled and the surface of the size.

Problem: Marbled fabric has a long, thin, white line across it.
Cause: A loose thread lay across the paint and blocked the color.
Solution: Trim threads on future fabric. For this piece, consider overmarbling.

Problem: The pattern is distorted by a line through it.
Cause: Hesitation mark; there was a break in the rhythm when the paper or fabric was laid on the size.
Solution: Lay the paper or fabric down in one smooth, continuous motion. (It's not a bad idea to practice on bare size before laying any paint.)

Problem: Marbled lines are fuzzy and wavy, rather than crisp and sharp.
Cause: The size is too thin, too young, or too old.
Solution: Thicken it, let it mature, or throw it out and start with a new batch.

Problem: The color won't take.
Cause: No alum or too weak an alum solution; or the pattern sat too long on the surface and sank; or sizing was left in the fabric.
Solution: Re-alum with a stronger solution; or work faster; or wash fabric more than once.

Problem: Color takes unevenly, leaving pale patches.
Cause: Too little alum or (ahem) too much.
Solution: Try a stronger alum solution; if the problem gets worse, try a weaker one.

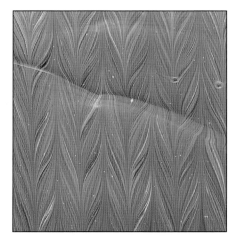 

Far left: This paper has two spectacular air bubbles. Center left: The small white dots were caused by dust that settled on the size. Center right: The same paper sports a hesitation mark. Far right: The thin white line on this fabric resulted from a stray end thread that lay across the fabric during marbling.

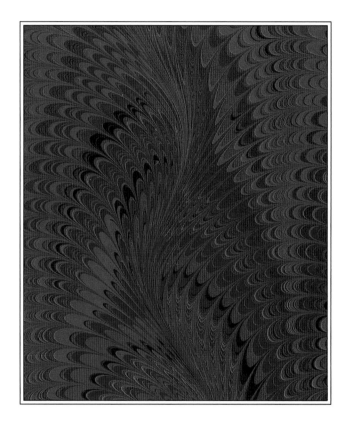

GLOSSARY

~~~~~~~~~~~~~~~~

If the moon is right, a stylus or rake can take on a life of its own, guiding your hand and allowing you to create spontaneous designs that delight you. But it's also satisfying to master the patterns that marblers have been using for centuries, to join the long tradition of the craft. This glossary includes just a few of those.

In the diagrams shown for each pattern, the proper tool is identified under each box. The solid arrows indicate the direction of movement, and the broken arrows represent the step just completed.

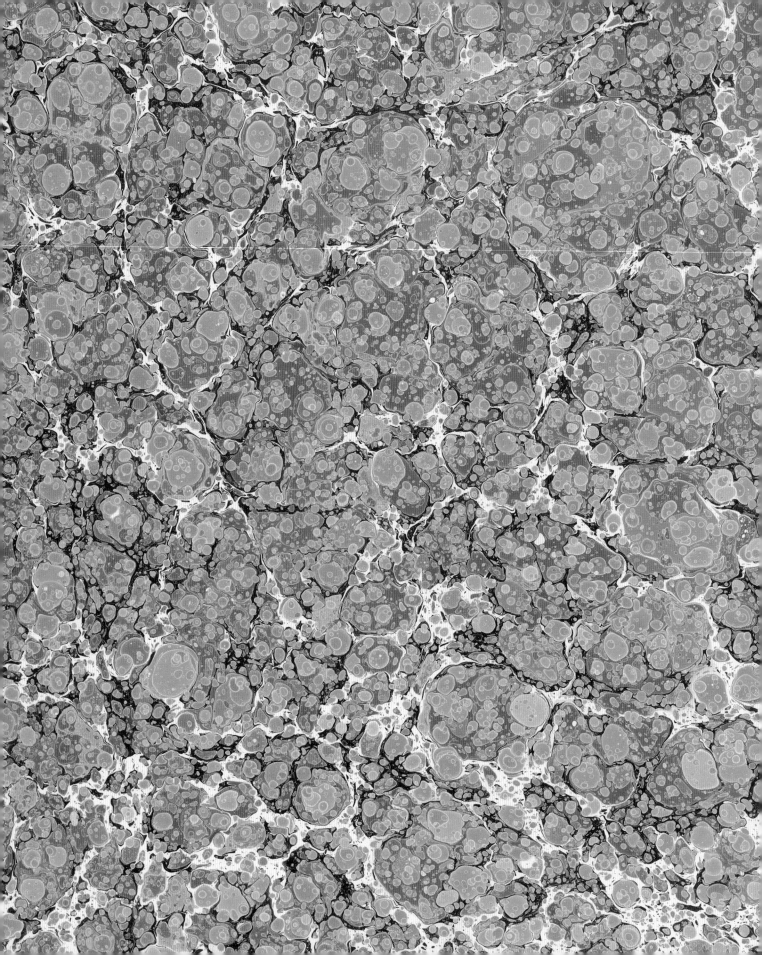

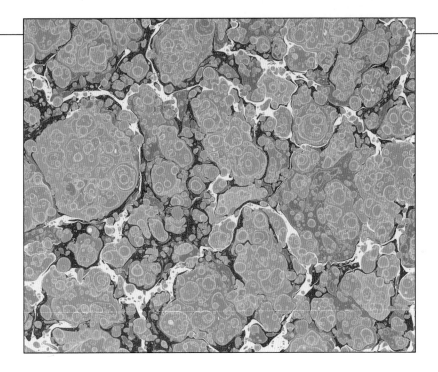

STONE

To make a stone pattern, apply drops of paint to the surface of the size until you are pleased with the colors and the pattern, and make the print. For the examples shown, extra ox gall was added to the paint to produce finer, narrower veins. Paint was applied with a whisk. Larger stones can be made with an eye dropper or, for fabric, with a plastic bottle. A stone pattern is the first step in all marbling patterns.

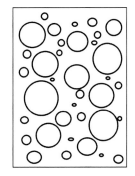

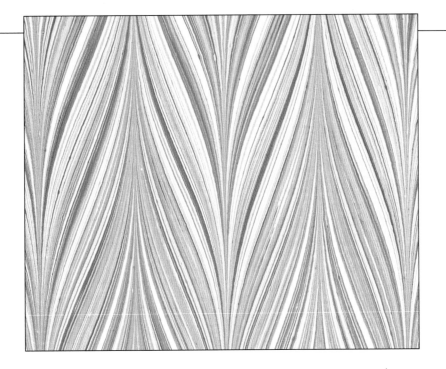

GET GEL

Get gel means "go and come" in Turkish, an apt description of this pattern, which forms the basis of most others. ("Get" is pronounced as it is in English; the *g* in "gel" is also hard.) The rake is drawn back and forth across the tray, first in one direction and then in the other.

A get gel pattern can be vertical or horizontal, depending upon the direction of the rake's pass. If you rake horizontally back and forth and then vertically up and down, you'll end up with a vertical pattern like the ones shown. If you rake vertically and then horizontally, you'll end up with a horizontal get gel.

Both get gels shown were made with a two-inch rake.

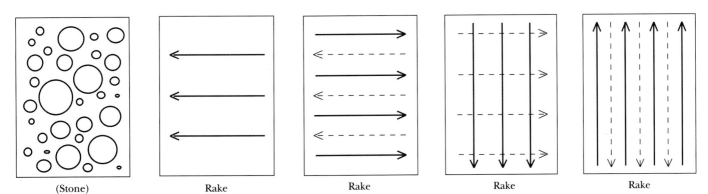

(Stone)   Rake   Rake   Rake   Rake

WAVED GET GEL

To wave the get gel, make a standard get gel, except for the final pass of the rake. In the final pass, instead of moving straight up the length of the tray, move the rake in a wavy, serpentine motion.

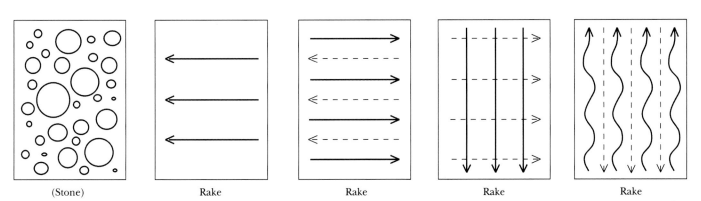

(Stone) Rake Rake Rake Rake

ZEBRA

A zebra pattern (which resembles the animal not at all) is simply a standard get gel with some stones on top. Adding a final round of stones to a pattern makes it "antique." Most patterns can be antiqued, for a different effect. Note that the added stones force the get gel lines apart, thus distorting the pattern somewhat, making it less linear, less precise. In the color scheme at left, the pattern evokes air bubbles rising from the bottom of the sea. In different hues, a zebra can be reminiscent of champagne.

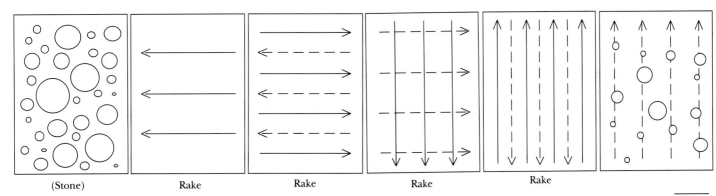

(Stone) Rake Rake Rake Rake

PEACOCK

Just as showy as the bird it's named for, the peacock pattern resembles a collection of peacock feathers. (Each loop represents a single feather.)

Start with a horizontal get gel – that is, rake vertically first, then horizontally. Then, using a bouquet comb, with its two rows of alternating teeth, comb down the length of the tray in a wavy "S" motion.

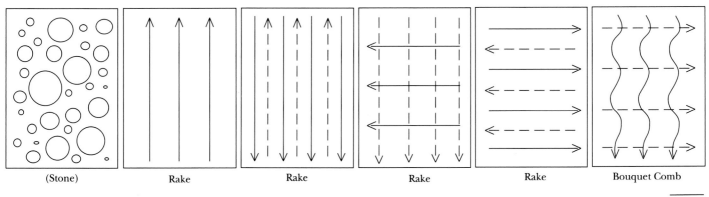

| (Stone) | Rake | Rake | Rake | Rake | Bouquet Comb |

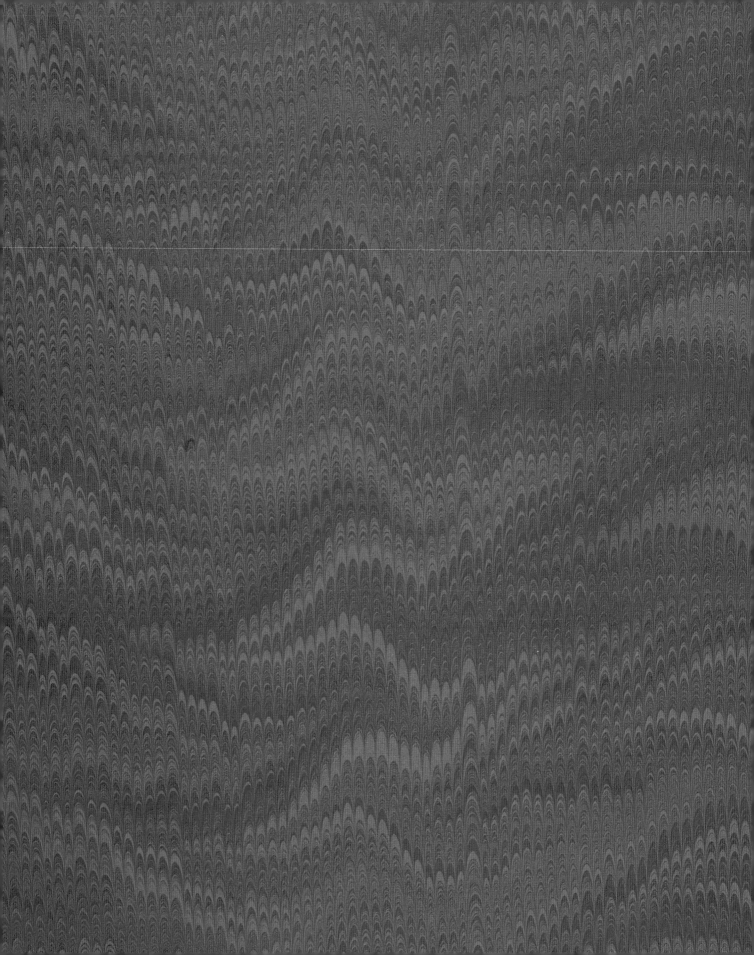

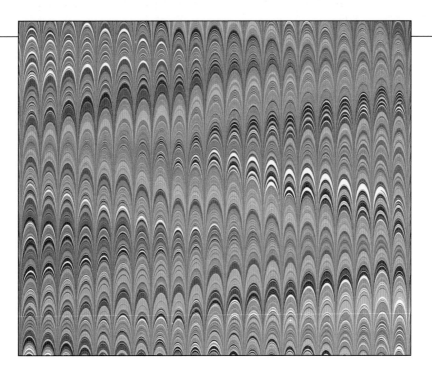

NONPAREIL

A combed get gel, the nonpareil is
the basis for endless variations. The
closer together the comb's teeth
are, the smaller the pattern will be.
The nonpareil at left was made with
a one-eighth-inch comb. The example above required teeth with
wider spacing. You'll want to comb
perpendicularly across the finished
get gel, so you'll need a horizontal
get gel pattern.

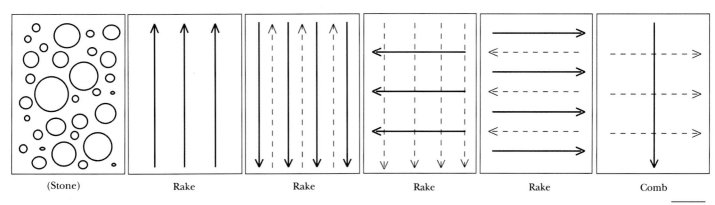

| (Stone) | Rake | Rake | Rake | Rake | Comb |

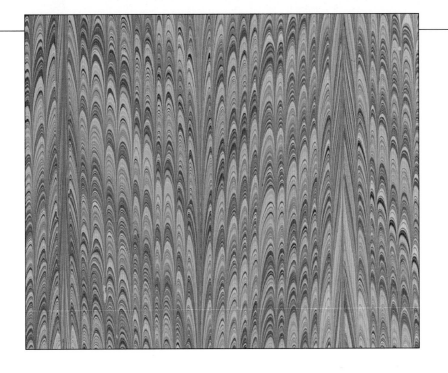

G O T H I C

To create a gothic pattern, make a nonpareil, then rake up and back down the length of the tray. The pattern at left was created with a two-inch rake, the one above with a three-inch rake.

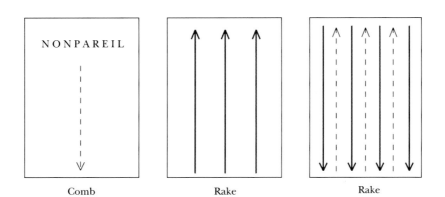

Comb   Rake   Rake

NONPAREIL

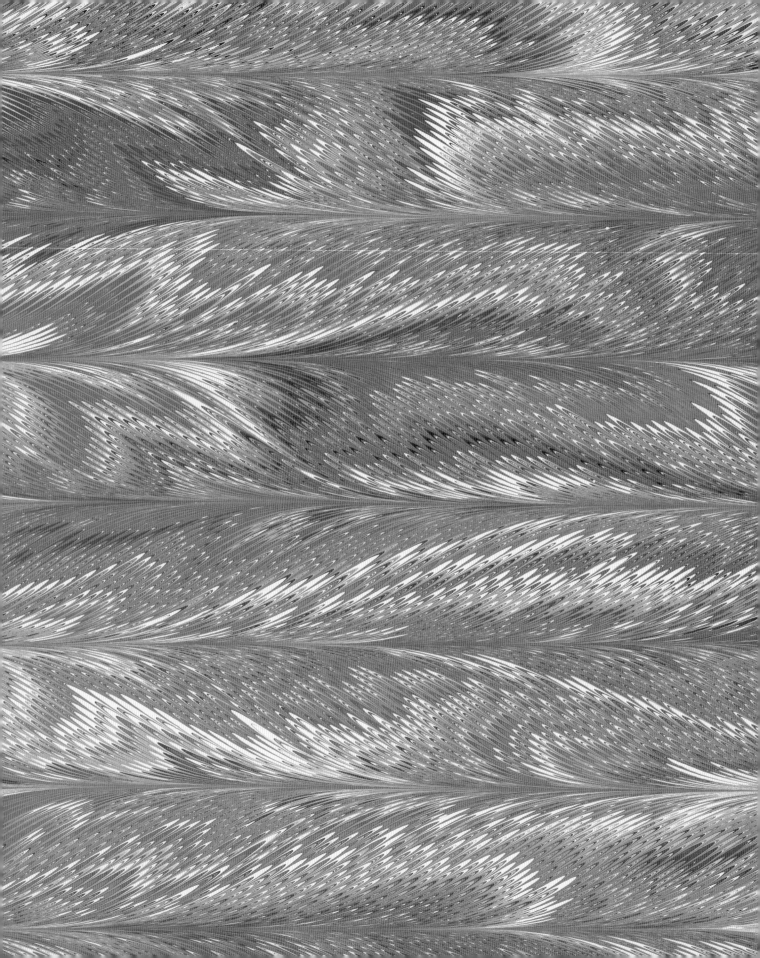

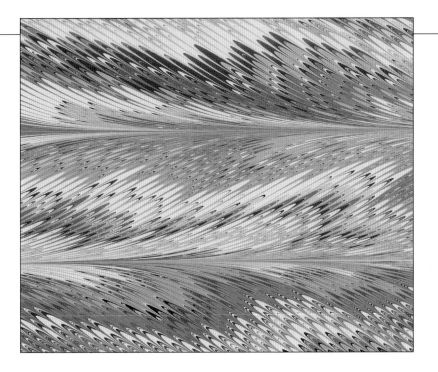

FEATHER

Like the gothic, the feather pattern is a raked nonpareil. But the feather is raked horizontally, rather than vertically.

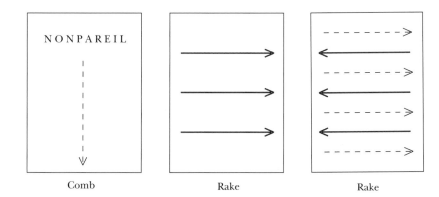

NONPAREIL

Comb   Rake   Rake

WAVED NONPAREIL

To create this fluid, motion-filled pattern, make a nonpareil, then pull a three-inch rake down the length of the tray in a gentle "S" motion.

NONPAREIL

Comb   Rake

BOUQUET

Like the peacock, the bouquet is
made with the bouquet comb. The
difference between the two patterns
is that the peacock is made on a
plain get gel; the bouquet is made
on a nonpareil.

To make a bouquet, create a
nonpareil, then move the bouquet
comb down the tray in a gentle "S"
movement. Note that the size of the
pattern can vary, depending on the
tools used.

NONPAREIL

Comb

Bouquet Comb

FRENCH CURL

Also known as "snail," this historic French pattern is another variation of the nonpareil. After creating a nonpareil (the large pattern at left was made with a quarter-inch comb, the sample above with a one-eighth-inch comb), use a rake to make the curls. Holding the rake along the vertical length of the tray, make small, tight circles with the teeth. A curl will form around each tooth. After you make one vertical row of curls, move over and make the next row, and so on until the pattern is complete.

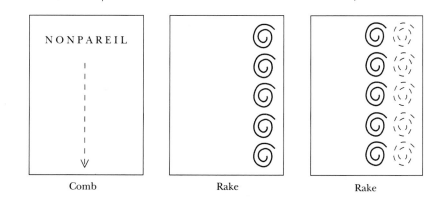

Comb   Rake   Rake

FREEFORM

Freeform marbling is limited only by your imagination. In both these samples, the artist made a nonpareil and then used a stylus to create free-flowing movement and curls. It's also possible to work freeform on a stone or get gel pattern.

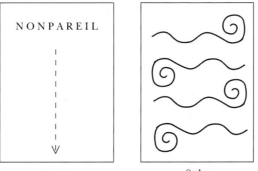

NONPAREIL

Comb   Stylus

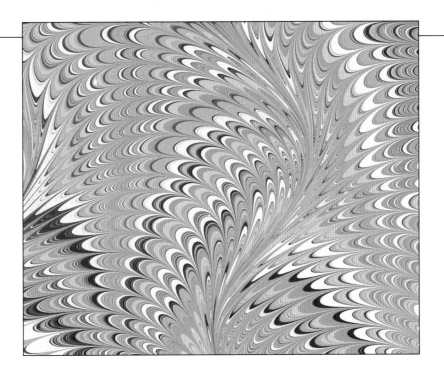

WAVED ICARUS

The only complication in this gorgeous pattern is that it is based on a horizontally combed nonpareil, rather than one made vertically. Thus it requires a comb that fits the length of the tray. Aside from that, it's a straightforward pattern. Make a vertical get gel, comb it horizontally, then wave down the length of the tray, using a three-inch rake and a wavy "S" motion.

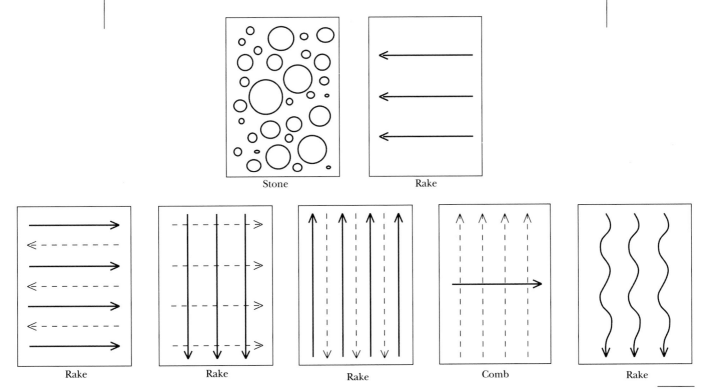

Stone

Rake

Rake

Rake

Rake

Comb

Rake

FEATHERED CHEVRON

This flame-like pattern relies on three different rakes: one with teeth three inches apart, one with teeth two inches apart, and one with teeth an inch apart.

Rake the stones horizontally back and forth with a three-inch rake, then vertically with a two-inch one, producing a vertical get gel. Now rake horizontally back and forth across the tray with a one-inch rake. Finish the pattern by raking vertically with a three-inch rake, with the final pass following a wavy "S" motion.

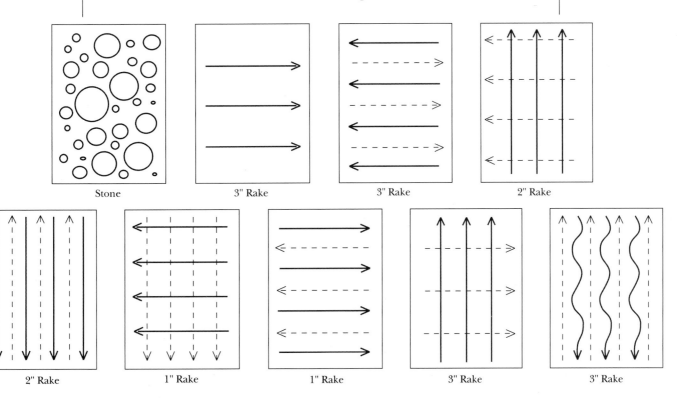

Stone   3" Rake   3" Rake   2" Rake

2" Rake   1" Rake   1" Rake   3" Rake   3" Rake

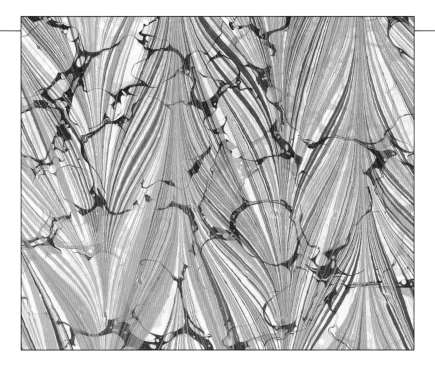

OVERMARBLING

Also known as "shadow marbling,"
overmarbling involves marbling a
piece of paper or fabric twice. After
the initial marbling, the item is allowed to dry, then remordanted and
marbled a second time. Overmarbling can be effective with a variety of
patterns and colors. The sample at
left consists of a one-inch get gel
over a feathered chevron. Above is
a get gel over a pattern of stones.

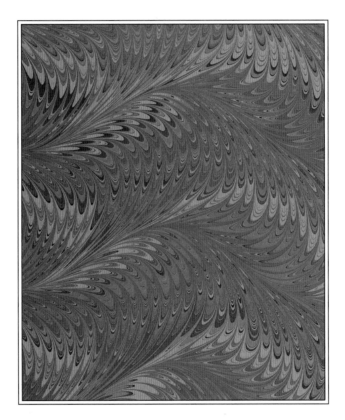

PROJECTS

At first it's enough to gaze at your newly marbled paper or fabric with the same fatuous approval usually reserved for a new baby. But sooner or later the desire to *make* something takes hold. The rest of this book offers suggestions and instructions for 36 ways to use your marbled goods.

Fabric can be marbled as yardage and then made into everything from vests to tablecloths. Another option is to marble an already finished item—a T-shirt, a silk tie, a canvas shopping bag. Paper almost always has to be marbled in sheets and then made into something as useful as it is decorative.

WEARABLE ART

FANNY PACK

Also known as a "hip pocket," a fanny pack leaves your hands free and your shoulders straight. Virtually everyone likes this comfortable and convenient carryall, and virtually everyone ignores both its names and wears it in front.

All of the major pattern manu-facturers include fanny packs in their pattern books. Just select a pattern and follow the instructions, with one notable exception. Make the adjustable belt longer than the pattern suggests. Apparently, professional designers are considerably more svelte than the population at large.

VEST

Marbled clothing can be a bit busy for some people. If you can't see yourself in an entire shirt or skirt of nonpareil, consider a vest. Worn with otherwise solid-colored garments, it will intrigue but not overwhelm.

The pieced vest shown combines blue marbled fabric with two different designs marbled in pink.

The panels are separated with strips of solid-colored fabric, and the vest is lined in hot pink.

Vests are among the easiest garments to sew—even easier if they are not pieced but cut from lengths of marbled fabric according to a standard pattern. All pattern books offer a variety of options.

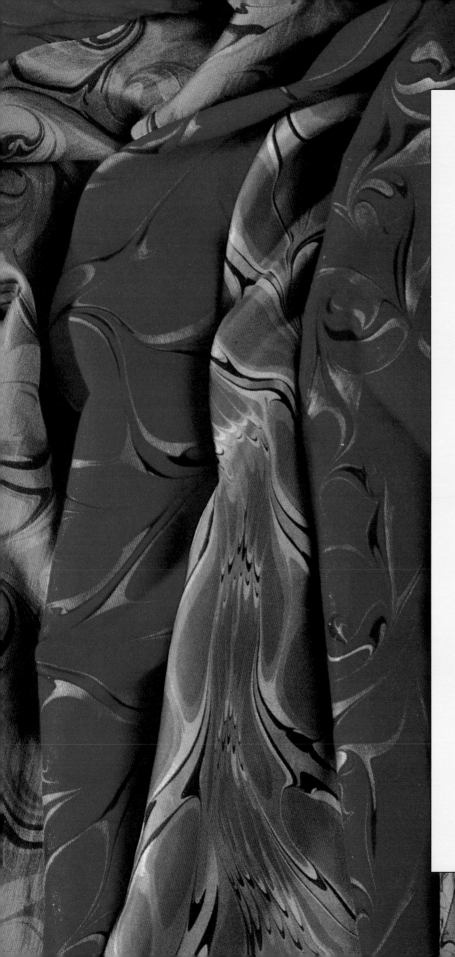

SCARVES

A marbled silk scarf is an elegant accessory. It's also a fairly uncomplicated project—a single thickness of supple cloth in a simple rectangular shape.

If the scarf is a small one, marbling it is a one-person task. Just stretch the ends taut as directed earlier, and proceed. If it's large—especially if it's long and narrow—you'll probably need to enlist a friend to help lay it on the surface of the size.

For the most spectacular results, start with a silk scarf in a vibrant color, readily available by mail and less expensive than one might think. The scarves shown here illustrate just how colorful the results can be. For a more subdued effect, start with a scarf in a more restrained color.

To care for a marbled scarf, hand-wash it in a pH-balanced shampoo; like hair, silk is a protein fiber. Press out excess moisture by rolling it up in a towel, then hang it to dry. Iron on the reverse side at a wool setting.

TENNIES

Tennis shoes are for life's carefree moments, so the more playful they look, the better. And nothing turns them wilder than marbling.

Buy shoes a size larger than usual (they'll probably shrink), soak them in an alum solution, and let them dry.

There are a couple of different ways to marble them. Probably the easiest is to submerge them. Use a bucket that's at least as wide as the shoes are long, and deep enough to allow the shoes to be completely covered with size. Fill the bucket with size, and make a pattern on the surface with acrylic fabric paints. Canvas has a lot of texture,

so fine patterns aren't likely to transfer well. Try a larger, free-form design.

Holding a shoe by the edges of the sole, lower it canvas-side-down into the bath, completely submerging it. The paint will wrap around the shoe, coloring both the front and the sides. Rinse it off, and set it aside to dry. Repeat the process for the other shoe.

A second method is to roll them. Using your regular marbling tray, make a pattern on the surface of the size with fabric paints. Hold a shoe canvas-side-down by the edges of the sole, and turn it so that one side of the shoe is facing down. Starting at one end of the pattern, roll the shoe from edge to edge across the surface, ending up in the middle of the pattern. Repeat for the other shoe, starting at the other end of the design and rolling it toward the center. Rinse and allow to dry.

For both methods, put the shoes through a clothes dryer for 15 minutes to heat-set the paint.

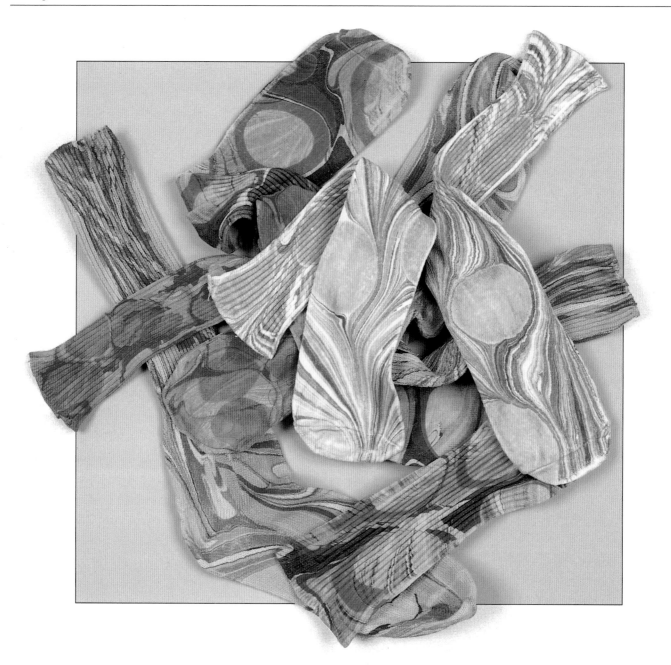

SOCKS

There's a plot afoot to stamp out tired, old socks. Goodbye gray and black. Hello stones and stripes!

You'll need a cardboard form to insert into each sock, to make it manageable and to prevent paint from bleeding through to the reverse side. Lay a sock on a piece of cardboard, with the heel flat against the board, and trace a rough outline of the sock. Now cut about 1/2" outside the lines, so that the form will stretch the sock during marbling, thus getting paint inside the ribs.

Insert the long, straight form so that the front of the sock is stretched flat. The least attractive parts of the finished sock will be along the edges of the form.

Now create a design on the bath. Starting at one end of the tray, lay a sock flat on the surface; then flip it over to color its reverse side. Then, starting at the other end of the bath, marble the other sock in similar fashion.

SHIRT & SUN VISOR

Plain tennis togs have gone the way of white tennis balls, and are missed just about as much. Even so, a marbled outfit might distract your opponent just enough to give you game, set, and match.

To marble the shirt, cut out a cardboard form large enough to insert inside the shirt. The form will stiffen the shirt, make it easier to handle, and prevent the paint from bleeding through to its opposite side. Create a design on the surface of the tray, and lay the front of the mordanted shirt on the paint. Skim the tray, lay a similar design, and marble the back.

The sun visor adds an additional complication: it's three-dimensional, rather than flat. The solution is a bucket that's as wide as the hat and deep enough to allow it to be submerged. Lay the paint on the surface, and slowly immerse the visor, top-side-down. The paint will wrap around the hat, marbling all sides of it.

ROMPERS

As useful as one-piece rompers are, their white, ribbed fabric is decidedly lacking in charm. A little marbling can make them almost as lovable as the baby who wears them.

Like other ready-made garments, rompers must be separated front from back during marbling. Otherwise, as the front is being marbled, some of the paint will bleed through to the back, leaving unsightly splotches. The easiest solution is to make a cardboard form to insert in the garment during marbling.

Just trace the romper's outline on a piece of cardboard, and cut it out. If the fabric is stretchy, make the form slightly larger, so that it will stretch the romper, thus allowing paint to cover the fabric thoroughly. Then create a one-of-a-kind garment for a one-of-a-kind baby.

T-SHIRTS

These days, when T-shirts go almost anywhere, you can marble one to match anything you own.

Colorful shirts are easy to do. You'll need to separate the front from the back while you marble; otherwise, paint will bleed through both layers and leave stains on the other side. Just draw an outline of the shirt on a piece of cardboard or posterboard, and insert it into the shirt. This not only allows for marbling one side at a time but makes the shirt easier to handle.

On a large tray, you can marble one side of the shirt at one end of the tank, flip the shirt over, and marble the other side on the rest of the same application of paint. If the tray is too small for that, just do the first side, skim the bath, and lay a second design. To be safe, leave the cardboard form in the shirt during rinsing, so that paint can't bleed through.

To marble a shape—for example, a heart—onto a shirt, again separate front and back with a cardboard form. Cut a heart out of a piece of heavy paper (the kind found in birthday cards). Lay the paints on the surface of the bath, and place the paper with the heart-shaped hole on top. Cover the rest of the tank with newspaper, and marble the shirt, making sure that the painted heart will end up where you want it. Be sure to leave the cardboard form in the shirt during rinsing.

You can reverse the design (that is, marble everything but the heart) by cutting a heart out of freezer-wrapping paper, and ironing the heart wax-side-down onto the shirt. Lay the paint on the size, and marble the shirt. After the paint is rinsed off, remove the paper heart.

To get a medallion effect, lay the paints in a small area in the center of the tank, make a design with a stylus, and lay the shirt on the paint.

MINISTER'S STOLE

To create this lovely ecclesiastical vestment, the marbler laid a pattern of carefully graduated pastels in a long, narrow tray and marbled a strip of fabric about 15" wide (38 cm.) and 60" long (150 cm.). The fabric was cut in half lengthwise to create the two sides of the stole (the sides thus match). The strips were lined with a solid-color fabric and joined at the neck. The finished stole is 56" long (140 cm.) and 4-3/4" wide (12 cm.) at the ends, tapering to 3-1/4" wide (8 cm.) at the neck.

BIKE PANTS

A commercial pattern and some raucous marbled fabric can produce a pair of pants any biker will love. The ones above probably qualify as a safety device—what driver could miss them?

Use a tight, stretchy fabric, such as cotton spandex or lycra spandex. Make sure to lay the pattern out so that the primary "give" is across, rather than up and down. Use the stretch stitch on the sewing machine, if possible, or use a longer than normal stitch and stretch the fabric as you sew.

For the pants above, first paint was laid on a tray in bands of bright color, and then swirled into a freeform design. After the fabric was marbled and dried, pattern pieces were laid out so that, in both front and back, stripes were in reverse order.

APRON

No one said a kitchen cover-up had to be boring. A simple home-sewn apron (all commercial pattern books offer several types) or a ready-made one can be marbled to match your counter tops or your attitude.

Cotton broadcloth is a good material. It's heavy enough to pro-tect your clothing from the sticki-est batter, and it accepts marbling well. Be wary of canvas. Although some types can be bullied into accepting marbling, many cannot.

To marble a large, odd-shaped garment such as this, you'll need to borrow an extra pair of hands to help lay it on the tray.

SHOPPING BAG

Since both paper and plastic grocery bags are harmful to the environment, many people are resorting to reusable cloth ones. Colorful marbling can make them attractive, as well as ecologically sound.

Plain canvas shopping bags are widely available. Although canvas is not the easiest material to marble, it can be done in most cases; just resign yourself to patterns that will be less than precise on this reluctant fabric.

Wash the bag two or three times, to rid the material of the repellent finish it probably has. Then mordant and marble it. You can enlist the aid of a friend to hold the bag taut as you marble first one side and then the other, or you can resort to a couple of the round cardboard tubes that come inside wrapping paper; they make excellent handles.

PILLOW

A throw pillow is one of the simplest ways to make use of marbled fabric, requiring only some polyester fiberfill and two pieces of fabric the same size. The pillow shown was made from two 20" (50 cm.) squares, one marbled and one solid, but there's no reason yours can't be rectangular and/or marbled on both sides.

Place the pieces of fabric right sides together, and pin in place. Beginning in the middle of one side, sew the pieces together with a 1/2" seam (13 mm.), leaving a 4" opening (10 cm.). Clip the fabric from the corners, and turn the pillow right-side-out through the opening. Press the pillowcase, and topstitch around the sides 1/2" (13 mm.) from the edge, again leaving the opening. Stuff the pillow with polyester fiberfill, making sure to fill the corners, for a good, plump shape. Blind stitch the opening closed, and topstitch the remaining 4" (10 cm.).

TABLECLOTH & NAPKINS

It's possible to sew strips of marbled fabric into a square (or circle) and thus become the proud owner of a marbled tablecloth. But it's also fun to marble a ready-made cloth on a single pattern. Cotton and cotton blends work well. Colored fabrics are excellent: if the cloth already has an interesting color and weave, you can apply paint to the bath more sparsely, allowing the fabric to show through. Napkins can be marbled to match.

If the tablecloth is too large for your tray, consider building a temporary one from some two-by-fours and clear plastic sheeting (see page 16 for directions).

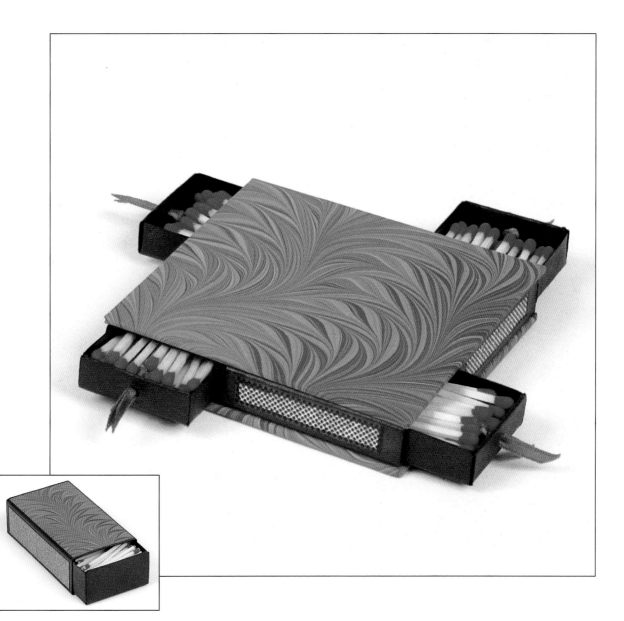

MATCH BOXES

Marbled paper can turn a plain box of matches into a striking accessory for your fireplace.

To dress up a large box of kitchen matches, just glue pieces of marbled paper to the front and back of the box, and blacken the edges and ends with a felt-tip marker. (The strike pads should be left untouched.)

Four small boxes of wooden matches can become a fine party favor with some marbled paper and some book board. Lay the boxes as shown, so that each can open to the outside. Cut two squares of book board large enough to cover the four match boxes (thin but heavy cardboard would also work). Glue marbled paper onto the coves, and allow them to dry under weights, about 24 hours. With a black felt-tip marker, dye the edges of the match boxes that will be visible, leaving the strike pads free. Punch a hole through one end of each box, and knot a short piece of ribbon through it to serve as a handle. Reposition the match boxes, glue the covers to the top and bottom of the boxes, and allow the entire assembly to dry.

NESTING ORIGAMI BOXES

Like most origami projects, these nesting boxes are more difficult to describe than to make. Each lid (and each bottom) is just a folded-up piece of paper. After you fold one, you can make others almost without thinking—during dull committee meetings, for example.

You can size the boxes to suit yourself; just cut the paper for the lid 1/4" (6 mm.) larger than the bottom. The three boxes pictured were made from marbled paper cut into the following squares: 8" and 7-3/4" (the lid and bottom of the large box); 7" and 6-3/4" (the medium box); and 6" and 5-3/4" (the small box).

1. On the wrong side of the 8"-square piece of paper, lightly draw pencil lines between opposite corners. Be accurate, or subsequent steps won't work.

2. Fold two opposite corners into the center, where the lines intersect.

3. Now fold in the other two corners, creating a new, smaller square (3a).

4. Fold one side of the square into the center. Then fold the opposite side to meet it.

5. Open the last two folds you just made. Now fold the other two sides in to the center in the same fashion as in step 4.

6. Open the last two folds; you've now got a square with creases. With scissors, make four cuts in the creases, as shown.

7. Unfold the long middle piece.

8. Lift the other two sides upright, and unfold their outermost folds, to form a box shape.

9. With double-sided tape, make an X across the bottom of the box.

Bring one of the long open pointed ends over the side of the box, and tuck the long pointed end into the bottom of the box. Smooth it down so it forms a seal with the bottom.

10. Repeat for the other long end.

You have just made the lid for the large box. The other lids and the bottoms are made in the same fashion.

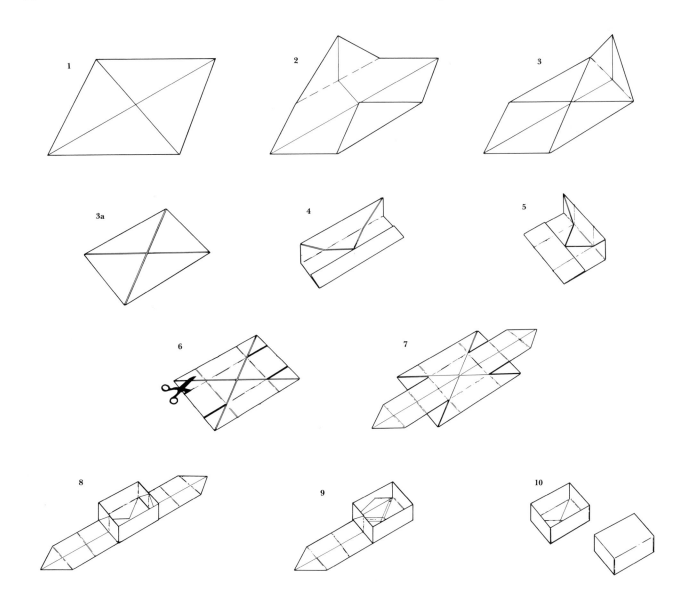

PLACE MATS

Because place mats are relatively small, they can handle vibrant colors and intricate designs that would be overwhelming in a tablecloth. Mats can be made entirely of marbled fabric (patterns for place mats are included in just about every pattern book). The ones shown here are enlivened by Seminole patchwork, which does an excellent job of using up small pieces of marbled fabric that are too pretty to throw away.

You'll need fabric for the mats themselves (in our case a red-orange cotton broadcloth); two contrasting strips of marbled fabric (ours are orange and yellow); and a narrow strip of a highlighting color (ours is purple). The amounts given are for two place mats.

Materials

Four 19" x 13" pieces of fabric (47.5 by 32.5 cm.), for front and back

Three 18" x 1-1/2" strips of marbled fabric (45 by 3.75 cm.), color A

Three 18" x 1-1/2" strips of a second marbled fabric, color B

Two 12" x 1" strips of a highlighter (30 by 2.5 cm.)

Thread to match the mats and the highlighter

Note: Strips of fabric longer than 18" (45 cm.) or so can be hard to work with in Seminole patchwork. That's why we've suggested six shorter strips of fabric, rather than four long ones.

Instructions

To construct the Seminole patchwork, pin a strip of marbled fabric color A to a strip of marbled fabric color B, right sides together. Sew strips together down one long side, using a 1/4" (6 mm.) seam. Press seam to darker side, and repeat for remaining strips.

Cut the strips crosswise into 1-1/4" pieces (30 mm.). Lay the pieces side by side, alternating their direction, to produce a patchwork effect. Right sides together, pin pieces together, and sew with a 1/4" (6 mm.) seam.

Fold a highlighter strip in half widthwise, wrong sides together, so that you have a 1/2" (13 mm.) strip 12" (30 cm.) long. Press closed.

Place the raw edge of the highlighter on a raw edge of the Seminole strip, and pin in place. Make sure the highlighter is pinned to the right side of the Seminole strip. Stitch with a 3/8" (9 mm.) seam and press open.

Position Seminole strip at desired angle on body of mat.

(Do the positioning with the right sides of both fabrics facing up, so that you can see what they will look like.) Holding the strip in position, flip it down, so that the right sides of strip and mat are together. Pin the strip in place along the edge without the highlighter, and stitch with a 1/4" (6 mm.) seam. Flip strip back up, and press. Pin the top edge of the strip in place, and topstitch along both edges of the highlighter.

Trim seams.

Place front and back of mat right sides together. Stitch around the mats 1/2" (13 mm.) from the edges, leaving an opening several inches wide so that you can turn the mat right side out. Clip corners, and turn mat. Press mat, and hand-stitch the opening closed.

Mark a faint line around the mat 2" (5 cm.) from the edges, and topstitch. Do not sew over Seminole strip. Repeat for other mat.

DISH TOWELS

Dish towels are excellent beginning projects. Small in size and regular in shape, they're easy to maneuver onto the surface of the tray. They're also child's play to make. Just cut out a piece of absorbent material to a desirable size, and narrow-hem it on all four sides. Even easier is purchasing a plain dish towel and marbling it—thus turning a forgettable item into a memorable gift.

WOODEN OBJECTS

Although paper and fabric are the most common materials, wood will also accept marbling. This hand-carved pine frog, which seems to have hopped straight out of an Amazon rain forest, and the Shaker boxes hint at the possibilities.

Like paper and fabric, wood must be mordanted first. These objects were dipped in a solution of 1/2 cup alum to one gallon of water (100 ml. to 3.8 liters), and then allowed to air-dry. A bucket wide and deep enough to contain the object was filled with methyl cellulose size, and a pattern in acrylic fabric paints laid on the surface. The item was then carefully lowered into the size, top-side-down, until it was completely submerged. The swirls of paint wrapped around it, marbling all sides. The Shaker boxes were marbled with their lids on, so that the paint would form a continuous pattern.

WASTEBASKET

If you'd care to wrap an entire wastebasket with marbled paper, just cut the paper to fit and paste it down. That's about as elegant as trash ever gets.

Another option is to create a collage from different papers, or even from scraps left over from other projects. Dummy up the collage, preferably on a surface that's about the same color as the wastebasket. When you're satisfied with the design, sketch it out on a sheet of paper, so you'll remember how it looked when you start transferring it to the basket piece by piece. Then paste the pieces up and glue them on.

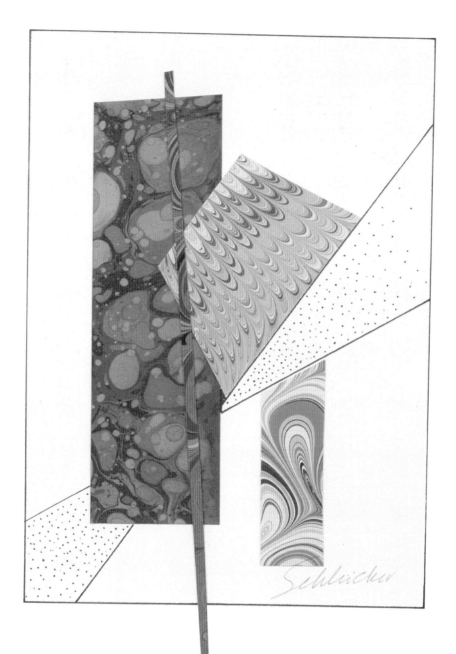

COLLAGE

Of course, it's not essential to make something out of every sheet of marbled paper. Many papers are quite lovely enough to be framed and hung on the wall. Even small pieces left over from other projects can end up in an interesting composition.

Collect all the scraps you haven't thrown away, including the ones you aren't very fond of (you never know). Lay them out on the table in front of you, and arrange and rearrange them until you like the effect. Paste them to a sheet of heavy paper, and ink in whatever lines, dots, or squiggles seem to be called for.

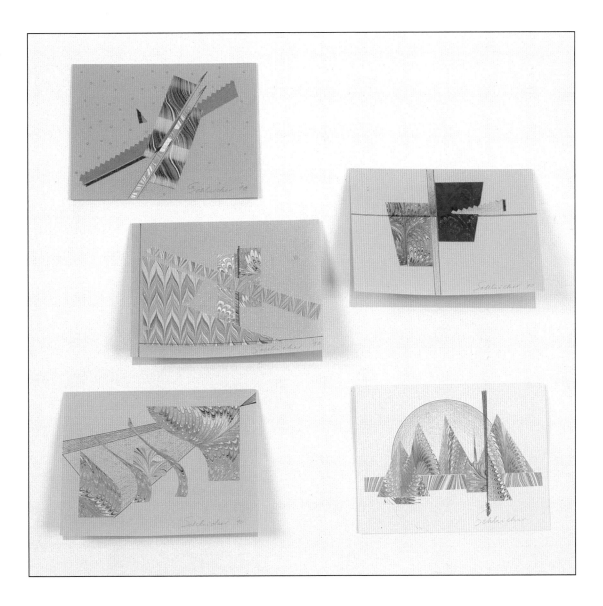

NOTE CARDS

Invitation, thank you, or apology, a note is remembered and appreciated when it comes on a distinctive marbled card. The cards on this page consist of plain, heavy paper folded in half and decorated with small pieces of marbled paper that are pasted on in pleasing arrangements. The designs are finished with an occasional piece of metallic paper and with a few lines drawn in black or metallic ink.

The notes on the next two pages started out as plain white cards with slightly recessed centers and matching white envelopes. Marbled paper was pasted over the center of the card, and a matching piece was cut to fit the raised flap and the back side of the envelope. To complete the envelope, slide the lining inside, and attach it just to the V-shaped flap with double-stick tape.

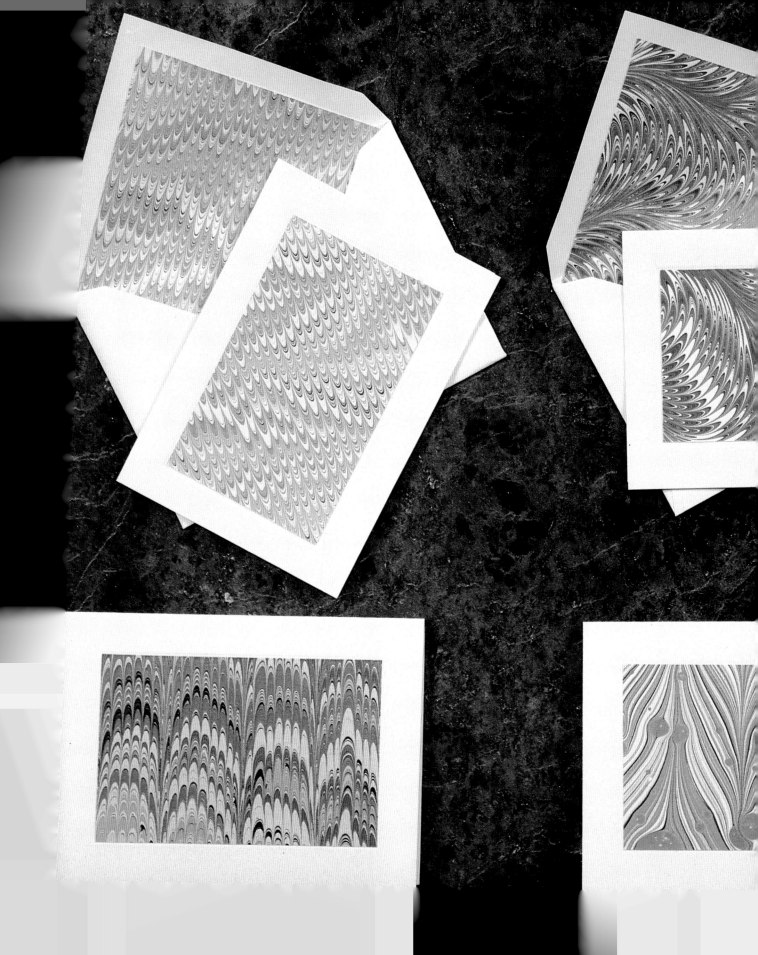

LEGAL PAD HOLDER

Anyone who takes notes, makes lists, jots thoughts, or sends memos will be delighted with this legal pad holder. It's useful, beautiful, and reusable—a new pad can be inserted after the first one is used up.

Although the finished project looks professional, it's not really difficult to make. You'll need some marbled paper cut into various sizes; some book boards (the stuff that makes hardback books hard); and some book cloth (the tough, flexible material that wraps around a book's spine and holds it together).

All you do is cut out a couple of book board covers, paste them together with a strip of book cloth, and paste some marbled paper inside and out.

Book cloth is available at some specialty shops or by mail. Book board is available from the same sources, or you can cannibalize used books; old textbooks can be had for next to nothing. Just cut off their covers, and tear off the paper or cloth attached.

Materials

One junior legal pad (standard 5" x 8" size)

Two 5-1/2" x 8-1/2" pieces of book board

Marbled paper:
- Two 5" x 9-1/2" pieces, for outside covers
- Two 5-1/4" x 8-1/4" pieces, for inside covers
- One 5" x 5" piece, for corner pocket (optional)
- One 4" x 12" piece, for sleeve to hold pad

- One 1-1/2" x 5" strip to decorate pad (optional)

Book cloth:
- One 5" x 9-1/2" piece, for outside spine
- One 2" x 8-1/4" piece, for inside spine

Fold the piece of book cloth for the outside spine in half down its length, to create a centerline.

Place the strip of book cloth on a piece of newspaper, and paste half of it, lengthwise. Lay a piece of book board on the pasted half of the spine, about 1/4" from the centerline (Figure 1). (You're leaving a little space in the center so that the spine will be able to wrap around the thickness of the legal pad and the two book boards.)

Paste the other half of the spine, and lay the other book board in place. Fold over the top and bottom of the spine, and press in place (Figure 2). Turn the book over, and smooth the spine onto the boards, making a tight, wrinkle-free bond.

Turn the book back over, with its inside facing up. Paste up the strip of book cloth for the inside spine, lay it in place, and smooth it down.

The next step is to cover the outside of the book with marbled paper. Turn the book over, with its outside up, and make yourself a guideline. To do that, measure 3-3/4" in from an outside edge (known in bookbinding as a "foredge"), and make a couple of light pencil marks. Using a ruler, extend the line the full length of the book. This will be your guide-

line for positioning the marbled paper. (The paper should overlap the book cloth spine by 1/4".) Place a ruler on the penciled line, and run the point of a bone folder gently (or other pointed tool) along its edge, so that you leave a shallow indentation.

Paste up a piece of marbled paper cut for the outside cover, and position it on the book, aligning it with the indentation on the spine. Cover the marbled paper with waxed paper, and smooth it down.

Turn the book over and cut off the paper's corners at a 45° angle, leaving a little surplus at the corners of the book (Figure 3). Fold over the paper at the top and bottom of the book, making sure the paper is tight against the board. Then fold the paper over the foredge of the book, and smooth it down.

Turn the book over, so the outside faces up. Place a ruler along the edge of the paper where it meets the book cloth. Gently press with the bone folder or another pointed tool, forcing the wet paper into the crease you made earlier (Figure 4).

Using the same steps, cover the other half of the book's outside.

Turn the book with its inside facing up. Paste up a sheet of the marbled paper cut for lining, glue it on the inside of the cover, and smooth it down (Figure 5). Repeat for other half of book. Cover the book with waxed paper, lay a flat board on top, and weight it down; leave it for 24 hours to dry.

If you choose to decorate the

legal pad itself, paste the decorative strip across the front of the pad, over the top, and down the back.

Fold pocket square as shown (Figure 6), marbled sides out. Then fold the margins over the lining, and trim off the protruding corners, so that you have a triangle. Paste up the folded margins, and paste the triangle together. Position the pocket in the lower left corner inside the book, leaving 1/8" margins at side and bottom, and glue in place. Weight down until dry.

Wrap the sleeve piece of marbled paper around the cardboard backing of the legal pad (Figure 7). Trim, if it's too long, so you have a 2" to 3" overlap, and paste it together, being careful not to paste it to the pad. Paste up the back side of the sleeve, and place it, pad and all, on the right inside cover of the book. Weight down until dry. The pad can be slipped out and replaced.

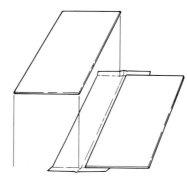

Figure 1

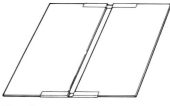

Figure 2

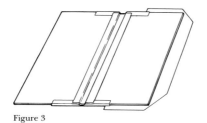

Figure 3

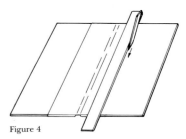

Figure 4

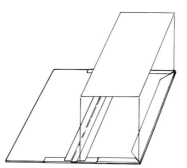

Figure 5

Figure 6

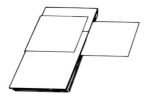

Figure 7

Metric Equivalent

1/8"	3 mm.
1/4"	6 mm.
1-1/2"	3 cm.
2"	5 cm.
3"	7.5 cm.
3-3/4"	9.37 cm.
4"	10 cm.
5"	12.5 cm.
5-1/4"	13.12 cm.
5-1/2"	13.75 cm.
8"	20 cm.
8-1/4"	20.6 cm.
8-1/2"	21.25 cm.
9-1/2"	23.75 cm.
12"	30 cm.

DESK SET

Elegant marbled paper and some craft glue can turn a few homey objects into a handsome desk set. Cover an orange juice can with marbled paper, and you have a pencil cup. Wrap ordinary pencils, and you have extraordinary ones. (Round pencils are easier, but hexagonal ones work too.) Find a suitable-sized box, cut a finger pull, cover with marbled paper, and you have a memo holder, just waiting for a stack of paper cut to fit.

The blotter must be built, but it's easy to do. Ours is 20" wide and 14" high (50 by 35 cm.), but the dimensions can be adapted for any desk top.

Directions

Glue the blotter paper on one side of the large piece of book board (now the front); the length of the

Materials

Book board:
- One 14" x 20" piece, for the bottom (35 by 50 cm.)
- Two 14" x 2-1/2" pieces, for the side panels (35 by 6.25 cm.)

Two 7" x 16" pieces of marbled paper (17.5 by 40 cm.)

One 20" x 16" piece of blotter paper (50 by 40 cm.)

One 13-1/2" x 19-1/2" piece of heavy paper, to cover back (34 by 49 cm.)

One 14" x 19" replaceable blotter, with corners trimmed (35 by 47.5 cm.)

paper should be vertical, so that you can turn the paper over the top and bottom of the board, but not around the sides. Cover a side panel with marbled paper: fold about an inch of the paper around the inside edge, and glue the folded portion and the portion on the top of the panel in place. Position the panel on the side of the blotter, and fold the marbled paper over the ends and the side of the blotter. Once fold lines are established, paste up the margins of the marbled paper, wrap it around the blotter again, and press in place. (The marbled paper will hold the side panel to the blotter.) Repeat for other side panel. Weight blotter with heavy objects so it will dry flat, and let dry 24 to 48 hours. Paste sheet of lining paper on back of blotter. Weight, and allow to dry. Add replaceable blotter, inserting the ends under the side panels.

ACCORDION FILE

You can get organized beautifully with this accordion file. It's a simple project. Just paste up a few pockets and sandwich them between two pieces of book board that you've covered with marbled paper.

The number and size of the pockets can vary. The file pictured has 12 made from card stock, a fairly heavy paper. For each pocket, take one sheet of paper and fold it in half end to end. Open the paper. On one half of the paper, trim 1/2" (13 mm.) from both sides; this will, in effect, cre-

ate two flaps on the other half. Fold the page again, on the same crease, and fold the flaps over the outside; the flaps will hold the pocket together. Paste the flaps, and complete the pocket. Make the rest of the pockets.

When the pockets are dry, join them together. To do that, brush a strip of paste about an inch wide (2.5 cm.) down the center of the outside of a pocket, line it up with another pocket, and press to seal. Then paste the other side of that one, and so on until the pockets are joined.

Don't attach the pockets at their outside ends; they should move freely.

Cut two pieces of book board slightly longer and wider than the pockets, and cover them with marbled paper. Weight the covers down, and let dry for 24 hours. When dry, cover the outside of an end pocket with paste, and attach the cover. The end of the pocket will become the lining for the book board. Repeat for other side. Cut a ribbon long enough to wrap around the accordion file, and glue it across the back.

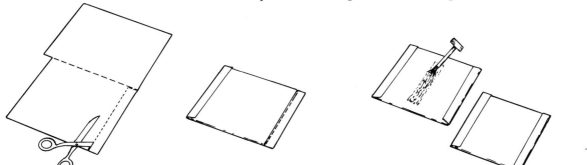

VALENTINES

No commercial Valentine, however funny or romantic, can compete with an original design crafted from marbled paper. Even a marbled sheet folded in half, with a heartfelt message on the inside, will remain tucked away long after other cards are gone.

For these handsome Valentines, small pieces of marbled paper were cut to form unique designs and pasted onto heavy,

colored paper: a marbled apple for the teacher, a flowerpot for Gramma, art deco cards for friends.

Cards can be cut to fit purchased envelopes, or envelopes can be made to fit the Valentines. An envelope is, after all, just a piece of paper folded and glued. Find a commercial one about the right size, unstick its edges, and use it for a pattern. Paste three sides of your new envelope together, insert the card, and paste the envelope closed. You can count on it: in any stack of mail, a marbled envelope will be opened first.

CHRISTMAS CARDS

How often have you vowed to make your own Christmas cards—only to discover that, come December, you're fresh out of cre-

ative ideas? This year, marble a stack of papers in brilliant Christmas colors, and send handsome, distinctive cards as joyous

as the season.

These cards consist of pieces of paper pasted together—some marbled, some plain, in various shapes, colors, and sizes. The cards with string attached were designed to do double duty. After they're opened and read, they can spend the rest of the season hanging on the Christmas tree.

BOOKS

Even our mundane thoughts seem profound when they're recorded in a homemade book. And they look even more impressive between marbled covers.

For a single-signature book in the traditional rectangular shape, you'll need only a dozen sheets of paper and a cover—a piece of marbled paper several inches wider than the book, so you can fold the extra margins under for a finished look.

Place the sheets of paper in a carefully aligned stack, and lay the sheet of marbled paper on top, right side up. Fold under the overhanging margins of the marbled sheet, leaving it about 1/8" (3 mm.) wider than the stack of paper on each side.

With a punch or a large needle, poke holes through all thicknesses of paper, as shown. A small book—say, 4" x 5" (10 by 12.5 cm.)—needs only three holes; larger books need five.

Thread a very large needle with heavy thread, and sew the book together as diagrammed. (Numbers indicate the path of the thread.) Tie a double knot, fold the book in half, with the stitches now forming the spine...and start writing.

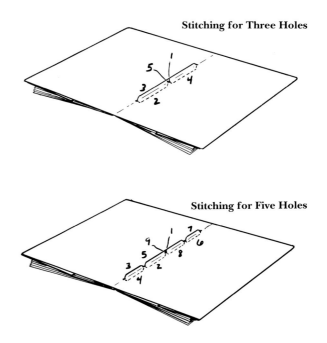

Stitching for Three Holes

Stitching for Five Holes

Numbers indicate the path of thread.

SMALL PAPER KITE

A soft breeze and a small kite—simple pleasures for a gentle afternoon. To make this kite, you'll need only an 8-1/2" by 11" sheet of marbled paper, a plastic trash bag, double-stick tape, and a ruler, pencil, and pair of scissors.

1. On the back (unmarbled side) of the paper, draw a centerline across the width of the paper, 5-1/2" from each end (Figure 1).

2. Measure 1-1/4" from the upper left corner, both along the top and down the side. Mark those two places, and draw a line between the marks. Repeat for upper right corner.

3. Along the centerline, mark 2-1/2" from top edge. Make a second mark 4-3/8" from the top edge.

4. At the top of the paper, make dots 3/8" to the right and left of center (Figure 2). At the bottom, make dots 3/4" to left and right of

center. Connect the dots on each side of the centerline.

5. Fold the paper along the centerline, with the wrong (unmarbled) sides together. Then fold along the angled lines to right and left of center—this time folding right sides together.

6. Slit the centerline between the 2-1/2" and 4-3/8" marks.

7. On the left fold, place a 2-1/2" piece of double-stick tape parallel to the slit (Figure 3). Pass the top left corner of the paper through the slit, as far as it will go, and press to make it stick.

8. On the right fold, place a piece of double-stick tape about 6" long parallel to the centerline; the tape should reach from the top of the paper to 2" from the bottom. Pass the top right corner through the slit, line it up with the left corner, and stick the kite together up and down the fold.

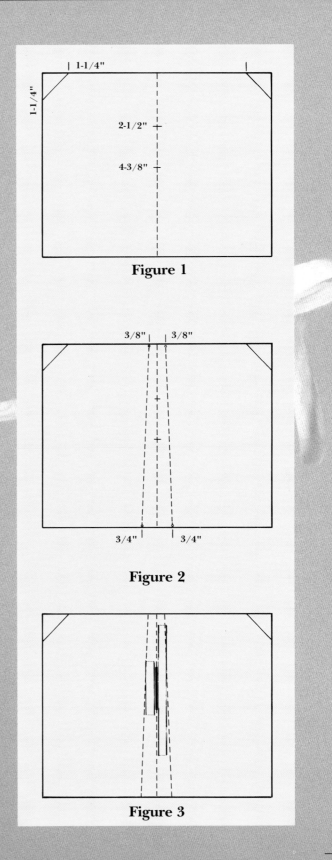

9. Punch a hole in the protruding triangle, so that string can be attached. Reinforce the paper triangle with transparent tape.

10. To make the tail, cut three long strips from a plastic kitchen garbage bag, each 1" wide. Stick the three strips together at one end with double-stick tape. Open up the back end of the kite (where it has not yet been taped), and place a piece of double-stick tape on each side of the fold. Sandwich the tail in between, and press closed.

Metric Equivalents

3/8"	9 mm.
3/4"	19 mm.
1-1/4"	30 mm.
2"	5 cm.
2-1/2"	6.25 cm.
4-3/8"	11.25 cm.
5-1/2"	13.85 cm.
8-1/2"	21.25 cm.
11"	27.5 cm.

MASKS

Masks are essential for ringing in the New Year. To make one, cut a pattern from scrap paper, and trace it onto marbled paper and onto a piece of poster board (or other backing). Cut both out, and paste them together. With a felt-tipped pen, outline the eyes and sketch in some lashes. If you like, punch a few holes on each side and tie on some complementary ribbons. For the handle, cut a slim dowel to a flirtatious length, and glue it onto one side.

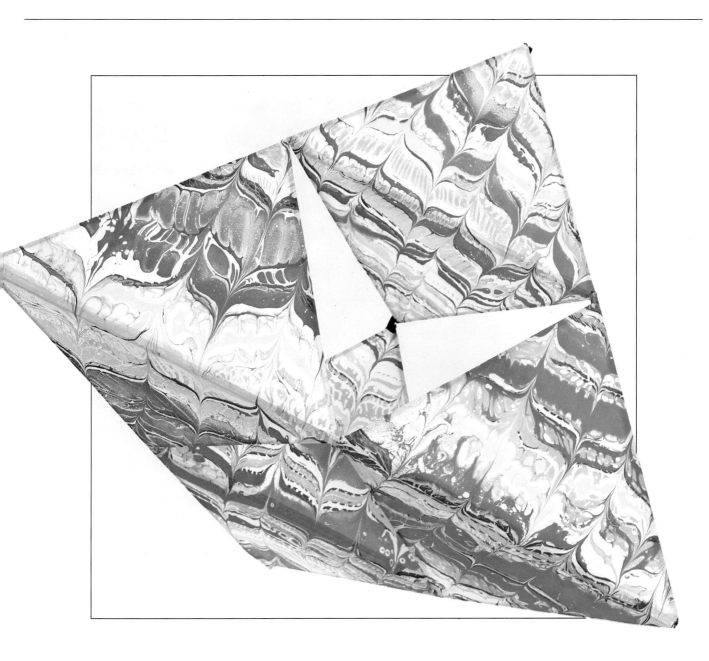

LARGE FABRIC KITE

This high-flying toy was invented by Alexander Graham Bell, during his investigations into manned flight, and is thus known as a Bell Tetrahedral Kite. It flies well in high winds—sometimes too well. During Bell's experiments, he tied several tetrahedrons together, to create a huge multicelled kite, and gave it to an assistant to hold. When a strong gust came along, the hapless assistant was lifted 30 feet (9 m.) into the air.

A Bell Tetrahedral is a spectacular sight when it's high in a blue sky—especially when it's covered in marbled fabric. For instructions on how to make it, see page 124.

JUMPING JACK & JILL

Movement is part of the charm of these loose-limbed toys. The arms and legs are loosely jointed, so that when the doll is at rest they hang more or less vertically (Figure 1). But pull its strings, and upper arms and thighs jerk into a horizontal position, with lower arms and calves swinging free (Figure 2).

These time-honored toys lend themselves to a large cast of characters. The ballerina and court jester shown here were constructed from fairly substantial marbled paper. Also required are some string and some very small brads.

For the ballerina, first enlarge the pattern pieces as desired, using a photocopy machine with that capacity. Cut out the pieces, and punch small holes where indicated by the dots. Glue the hair onto the head, and the dress onto the body. Weight the doll down, and allow to dry. Using the tiny paper brads, attach lower arms to upper arms, and calves to thighs. Now attach arms and legs to body, and draw the face. Make sure that all joints move easily. If they stick, separate the parts and enlarge the holes.

String the doll as shown in Figure 1. Make a hole at the top of each arm, above the brad, and join the two arms with a length of string. Tie the string just tight enough so that it is horizontal when the arms are hanging down. When you pull down on the center of the string with your fingernail, the two arms should rise (Figure 2). If the string is too loose, you'll merely take up its slack. If it's too tight, the legs will already be raised before you tug at all.

Punch holes in the upper thighs, and join them as you did the arms. Now add the operating string. Tie it to the center of the arm string and to the center of the leg string, leaving enough to hang below the body. If you'd like, thread a wooden or metal bead onto the bottom, and tie a knot just beneath it, to hold it on. When you pull the operating string, it will bring arms and legs to life. Loop a string through the top of the head, to hold onto when you jerk its strings.

The jester is very similar. Just paste the body/helmet piece onto the backing/face piece, and weight down until dry. Then assemble the jumping jack as described above.

Figure 1

Figure 2

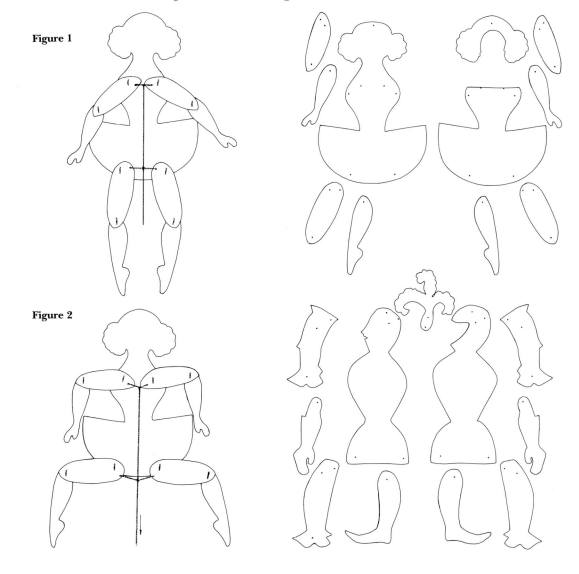

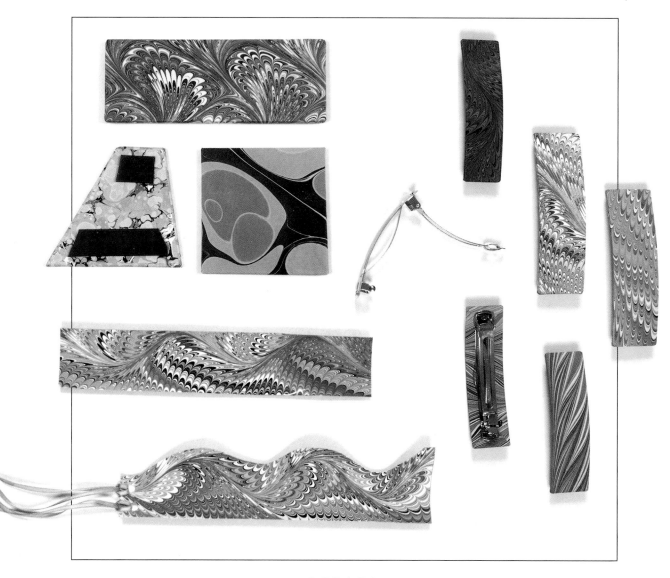

SCRAPS

There are lots of ways to use the scraps of marbled paper too pretty to throw away. Declare one sliver a bookmark. Turn a second scrap into a refrigerator magnet: just paste it over a piece of book board and attach strip magnets (available at craft stores) to the back with epoxy. Or make an eye-catching barrette with book board, epoxy, and a barrette clip (available in fabric stores or by mail-order).

Cut two pieces of book board just a hair longer than the clip (1/4" to 1/2" longer, or 6 to 13 mm.) and whatever width you want the barrette to be. Set one piece aside for later. Cover the other with marbled paper, and let dry.

Hold the extra piece of book board against the right side of the covered barrette, and gradually bend the barrette into an arc, to match the arc of the clip. Mix the

two parts of the quick-drying epoxy, following manufacturer's instructions, and dab some on the back of the clip—at each end and in the middle. Glue the clip to the barrette, protect the front with the extra piece of book board, and clip all three pieces together with a plastic clothespin or a spring clip. (Wooden clothespins will leave a little bit of themselves behind.) Let dry about half an hour.

HOW TO PASTE

No matter how you decide to use your marbled paper, you'll probably end up pasting it to something. Once in a while double-sided tape works as well or better (on note cards, for example), but mostly you'll paste. Even if you've been happily sticking things together since kindergarten, a few grown-up tricks of the trade can help.

Materials

First, there's the *paste*—white craft glue available just about any-place. Thin it with water or dilute it with some methyl cellulose size (60-40 glue-to-size). Some craft glues are more flexible when dry, and these are preferable. Check with your retailer for recommendations.

You'll need a *brush*—a 1-1/2" or 2" (or even larger) varnish brush (4 or 5 cm.) works well. If you size the brush to the project (large brushes for large expanses of paper), the pasting will be easier and the coat will be more even.

You'll also need a *ruler*, a *pencil*, some *waxed paper*, and a stack of 10 or 12 sheets of *newspaper* (if they're at least three months old, the ink won't rub off).

A *bone folder* is an incredibly useful little tool. It's usually made of bone, and its purpose is to help you fold. To use it, lay a ruler on the paper, with its edge where you want the fold to be. Bracing the bone folder against the ruler, use the point to score a line where you want the fold to be. Now you can make a smooth, even fold along the crease. The folder is also useful for smoothing pasted paper to create a tight, wrinkle-free seal, and for making small tucks at the corners of a project.

You'll also need a *press board*—a thin, hard board to cover the paper and support books or other heavy weights. Pasted items need to be weighted while they dry; otherwise, they'll curl. A press board protects the pasted paper and distributes the weight evenly.

Instructions

1. Pasting needs to be done quickly; otherwise the paper begins to dry out, which produces an uneven seal and a wrinkled surface. It's helpful to cut all the materials to size before beginning to paste.

2. Place the paper, marbled side down, on a stack of newspaper, and brush on a thin, even coat of paste. Avoid back-and-forth brush strokes. Start in the center of the paper, and brush outward, over the edges of the paper. If you brush back over the edge toward the center, paste will get on the decorated side of the paper.

3. If the paper begins to curl as you paste, just continue the pasting; as it gets wetter, it will relax.

4. If you get too much paste on the paper, brush it outwards onto the newspaper. You're aiming for a thin, even coat that will not squish out around the edges as you smooth the paper in place.

5. When the paper is pasted, lift it by one corner and remove the top sheet of newspaper (which is now covered with paste). Replace the pasted paper on the now-clean stack of newsprint, and continue with the project.

6. Working quickly, place the pasted paper in position, wherever you want to glue it. Cover it with a sheet of waxed paper, and smooth it down with the bone folder: holding the bone folder horizontal, scrape its long edge firmly across the surface, for a tight, wrinkle-free seal.

7. Whenever paper is pasted to book board, the board will try to curl. You can thwart it by "countering"—pasting another sheet of paper to the other side of the board. Any finished project must be countered if it isn't to curl later.

8. Cover the pasted paper with the press board, stack weights on top, and allow to dry—which will take 24 to 48 hours.

Be sure the press board is clean. Wet paper is very fragile and easily torn or soiled. It will bear the permanent imprint of any grit or foreign material that gets pressed into it.

—*Patty Schleicher*

This spectacular kite isn't as difficult to construct as it might seem from a quick glance at Figure 1, which shows the kite's wooden skeleton before it's covered with fabric. Probably the easiest way to start is to collect some small sticks, some scraps of paper, and a little paste or tape, and play with a small model. After you've got the concept, the actual building is easy.

Materials. You'll need some lightweight square wood a quarter inch (6 mm.) in diameter to serve as the spars—the rigid sticks that hold the cloth rigging; some lightweight marbled fabric for the covers; small, thin nails; glue; thin plywood for the corner-pieces; tape; a small wooden or plastic ring; and some sturdy kite string.

Instructions. Cut seven spars 56" long (140 cm.) and 12 spars 28" long (70 cm.) Miter both ends of all spars at a 30° angle (Figure 2).

Lay out three long spars in a triangle, with their mitered ends together (Figure 3). Glue the ends together. Cut triangular cornerpieces of thin plywood, and nail them to the corners (Figure 4). Make a second triangle from long spars in the same manner.

From six small spars, assemble two small triangles to act as braces (Figure 5) and attach them to the main frame as shown (Figure 6).

Build two more triangles from the remaining short spars; these are hinge triangles. Take one hinge triangle, lay one side of it on the crosspiece of a main

frame's bracing triangle (Figure 7), and attach with glued cloth hinges (Figure 8). Repeat for remaining hinge triangle and frame. Now join the two large triangular frames together (see Figure 7) with glued cloth hinges.

Stand the assembly on its side, and fold the two frames forward to make two sides of a pyramid, with the hinge flaps on the inside. Join the bottom of the pyramids with the last long spar and tape securely at both corners (Figure 9). Bring the free corners of the hinged triangles together and tape to the center of the long spar. Later, these tapes can be undone and the long spar removed, allowing the kite to lie flat for travel.

Cut out the fabric covers (Figure 10) and attach them to all triangles except the central one in each main frame. Attach the cover by turning the edges around the spars and gluing in place (Figure 11). The third side of the pyramid is left open (Figure 12). Attach the kite string as shown in Figure 13.

Figure 1

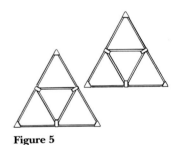

Figure 5

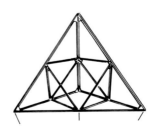

Figure 9

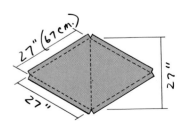

Figure 10

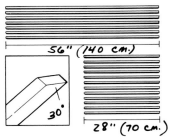

Figure 2

56" (140 cm.)

30°

28" (70 cm.)

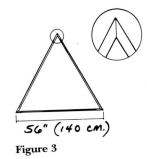

Figure 3

56" (140 cm.)

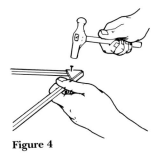

Figure 4

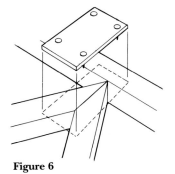

Figure 6

Figure 7

Figure 8

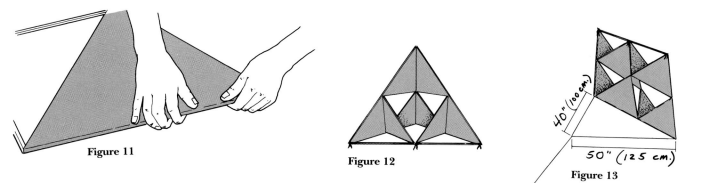

Figure 11

Figure 12

Figure 13

40" (100 cm.)

50" (125 cm.)

Patty Schleicher studied art and anthropology, but her love of books—their look, feel, and smell—led her to become a librarian. When she chanced upon some old books with marbled end papers, she taught herself to marble (from books, of course) and became a full-time marbler in 1980. She markets her work primarily through craft fairs, and has taught innumerable workshops.

Patty's projects in this book include the vest (page 77), the minister's stole (page 87), the wastebasket (page 99), the collage (page 100), both sets of note cards (pages 101-103), the desk set (page 104), the accordion file (page 105), the legal pad covers (page 106), the sewn books (page 114), and the jumping jack and jill (page 120).

Mimi Schleicher (daughter of Patty) studied ceramics and weaving, but she became a full-time marbler four years ago, the day she pitched in to help her mother meet a production deadline. The two women have been in business together ever since.

Mimi's marbling appears on the cover, the end papers, the title page, and the table of contents; on the chapter openings on pages 8, 12, 42, and 74; on the clothesline, pages 28-29; and throughout the glossary of patterns (pages 44-73). Also hers is the suminagashi on page 11. She appears marbling paper on pages 32-33.

Her projects include the match boxes (page 93), the origami boxes (page 94), the Valentines (page 110), the Christmas cards (page 112), the masks (page 118), and the inventive uses for scraps (page 122).

Laura Sims first became interested in marbling when she drove cross-country with a friend who talked about *nothing* but the workshop she'd just taken from Patty Schleicher. A former Spanish and biology teacher, Laura became a full-time marbler in 1986, when she started a business called Indigo Stone. She regularly teaches marbling. Her oldest student so far was 76; her youngest, three. She is seen marbling fabric on pages 36-37.

Laura's projects include the silk scarves (page 78), the tennies (page 80), the socks (page 82), the T-shirts (page 86), the apron (page 89), the pillow (page 91), the tablecloth and napkins (page 92), the place mat and napkin (page 96), the dish towel (page 97), the wooden frog and Shaker boxes (page 98), the small paper kite (page 116), and the large fabric kite (119).

Carol and Carolyn Cullen (mother and daughter) first encountered marbling when Carol happened upon an exhibit of Patty Schleicher's work. Carol drove home and announced, "This you've got to see." Both women drove back to the exhibit, and decided that they had found their craft. They taught themselves to marble (from books) and began a business called Cullen Color.

The Cullens' projects include the fanny pack (page 76), the bike pants (page 88), and the shopping bag (page 90).

And thanks to...
Hans Schleicher, husband of Patty and father of Mimi, a woodworker who stopped making marbling trays for his wife and daughter long enough to marble the Pixie face on page 14; John Hillyer, an accomplished woodcarver, who carved the pine frog on page 98; Pam Cauble, who designed and made the place mats on page 96; Kay Pool, proprietor of Basquettes, in Asheville, North Carolina, who designed the mask arrangement on page 118; and Pat Wald, who parted with her beloved tennis racket for a full 12 hours (page 83).

BIBLIOGRAPHY

Chambers, Anne. *The Practical Guide to Marbling Paper.* New York: Thames and Hudson, 1986.

Cohen, Daniel, and Paula Cohen. *Marbling on Fabric.* Loveland, Colorado: Interweave Press, 1990 (94 pages).

Easton, Phoebe. *Marbling: A History and a Bibliography.* Los Angeles: Dawson's Book Shop, 1983 (190 pages).

Fox, Polly. *Marbling on Fabric.* Taos, New Mexico: Fresh Ink Press, 1990 (40 pages).

Guyot, Don. *Suminagashi: An Introduction to Japanese Marbling.* Seattle: Brass Galley Press, 1988 (22 pages).

Ink and Gall, a biannual journal for marblers, is available for $35 a year (includes two newsletters) from Ink and Gall, Box 1469, Taos, NM 87571.

Lewis, A. W. *Basic Bookbinding.* New York: Dover Publications, 1957 (144 pages).

Mauer, Paul, and Diane Philippoff Mauer. *An Introduction to Carrageenan and Watercolor Marbling.* Self-published, 1984 (24 pages). Available from Diane Maurer, P.O. Box 78, Spring Mills, PA 16875.

Nevins, Iris. *Fabric Marbling.* Self-published, 1985. Available from the author, Rt. 3, Box 613, Sussex, NJ 07461.

Nevins, Iris. *Traditional Marbling.* Sussex, New Jersey: Self-published, 1988.

Schleicher, Patty. *Oil Color Marbling.* Self-published, 1984 (16 pages). This introduction to marbling with oil colors is available from the author, P.O. Box 1005, Weaverville, NC 28787.

Shannon, Faith. *Paper Pleasures.* New York: Weidenfeld and Nicholson, 1987 (168 pages). A good source for paper projects.

SOURCES OF SUPPLY

For a marbler, mail-order suppliers are essential. Although some supplies, such as acrylic fabric paints, are available almost everywhere, necessities such as ox gall, carrageenan, and book board are not. The following sources carry either some or all of the materials required.

Colophon Book Arts Supply
3046 Hogum Bay Rd. N.E.
Olympia, WA 98506
(206) 459-2940

Color Craft
14 Airport Park Rd.
E. Granby, CT 06026
(800) 243-2712

Decorative Papers
P.O. Box 749
Easthampton, MA 01027
(413) 527-6103

Earth Guild
33 Haywood St.
Asheville, NC 28801
(800) 327-8448

Diane Maurer
Box 78
Spring Mills, PA 16875
(814) 422-8651

Talas
213 W. 35th St.
New York, NY 10001-1996
(212) 465-8722
(catalog $5.00)

Thai Silks
252 State St.
Los Altos, CA 94022
(800) 722-SILK
(Silk scarves in a variety of sizes.)

United Notions
5560 Fulton Industrial Blvd.
Atlanta, GA 30336
(404) 344-7027
(Barrette clips.)

INDEX